GOD
CAME NEAR

GOD
CAME NEAR

CHRONICLES OF THE CHRIST

Max Lucado

Multnomah Publishers *Sisters, Oregon*

GOD CAME NEAR
published by Multnomah Publishers, Inc.
© 1986 by Max Lucado

International Standard Book Number: 1-57673-387-4 (hd)
                                         1-57673-386-6 (pa)

Printed in the United States of America
Cover photograph by: Marc Norberg
Cover design by: Stephen Gardner

Unless otherwise indicated, Scripture quotations used in this book are from *The Holy Bible,* New International Version (NIV) © 1973, 1984 by International Bible Society, used by permission of Zondervan Publishing House.

Also quoted: *The Holy Bible,* New King James Version (NKJV) © 1984 by Thomas Nelson, Inc.

Revised Standard Version Bible (RSV) © 1946, 1952 by the Division of Christian Education of the National Council of the Churches of Christ in the United States of America.

The Living Bible (TLB) © 1971. Used by permission of Tyndale House Publishers, Inc. All rights reserved.

The New Testament in Modern English, Revised Edition (Phillips) © 1972 by J. B. Phillips.

The New Jerusalem Bible © 1985 by Darton, Longman & Todd, Ltd. and Doubleday & Company, Inc.

The Good News Bible: The Bible in Today's English Version © 1976 by American Bible Society.

Library of Congress Cataloging-in-Publication Data
Lucado, Max
   God came near.
      1. Incarnation—Meditations.   I. Title.
BT220.L82   1987   232.'1   87-12502
ISBN 1-57673-387-4 (hd)
ISBN 1-57673-386-6 (pa)

99 00 01 02 03 04 — 48 47 46 45 44

To Steve and Cheryl Green
"A faithful friend is a sure shelter,
whoever finds one has found a rare treasure."

ECCLESIASTICUS 6:14

"Sir," they said, *"we would like to see Jesus."*

JOHN 12:21

"We were eyewitnesses of his majesty."

2 PETER 1:16

CONTENTS

Part II
Our Imitation
"A student...who is fully trained will be like his teacher."

ACKNOWLEDGMENTS

My deepest thanks to:
Liz Heaney and the Multnomah staff:
they don't come any better.

Jim Woodroof, Rubel Shelley, Richard Rogers and
Joan Carrigan (my sister):
your encouragement and suggestions were invaluable.

Carl Cope:
what would I do without your eleventh hour aid and
twenty-four hour friendship?

The Rio team:
amigos queridos!

Stanley Shipp:
you're one of the finest men on earth.

The elders of the Highland Church of Christ:
I appreciate the pastoral care and prayers.

And most tenderly, thank you, Denalyn:
If a star fell each time I thought of you, the sky would be empty.

Eyewitnesses of His Majesty

*Christianity, in its purest form, is nothing
more than seeing Jesus.
Christian service, in its purest form, is nothing
more than imitating him who we see.
To see His Majesty and to imitate him,
that is the sum of Christianity.*

For fifty-one years Bob Edens was blind. He couldn't see a thing. His world was a black hall of sounds and smells. He felt his way through five decades of darkness.

And then, he could see.

A skilled surgeon performed a complicated operation and, for the first time, Bob Edens had sight. He found it overwhelming. "I never would have dreamed that yellow is so...yellow," he exclaimed. "I don't have the words. I am amazed by yellow. But red is my favorite color. I just can't believe red.

"I can see the shape of the moon—and I like nothing better than seeing a jet plane flying across the sky leaving a vapor trail. And of course, sunrises and sunsets. And at night I look at the stars in the sky and the flashing light. You could never know how wonderful everything is."

He's right. Those of us who have lived a lifetime with vision can't know how wonderful it must be to be given sight.

But Bob Edens isn't the only one who has spent a lifetime near something without seeing it. Few are the people who don't suffer from some form of blindness. Amazing, isn't it? We can live next to something for a lifetime, but unless we take time to focus on it, it doesn't become a part of our life. Unless we somehow have our blindness lifted, our world is but a black cave.

Think about it. Just because one has witnessed a thousand rainbows doesn't mean he's seen the grandeur of one. One can live near a garden and fail to focus on the splendor of the flower. A man can spend a lifetime with a woman and never pause to look into her soul.

And a person can be all that goodness calls him to be and still never see the Author of life.

Being honest or moral or even religious doesn't necessarily mean we will see him. No. We may see what others see in him. Or we may hear what some say he said. But until we see him for ourselves, until our own sight is given, we may think we see him, having in reality seen only a hazy form in the gray semidarkness.

Have you seen him?

Have you caught a glimpse of His Majesty? A word is placed in a receptive crevice of your heart that causes you, ever so briefly, to see his face. You hear a verse read in a tone you'd never heard, or explained in a way you'd never thought and one more piece of the puzzle falls into place. Someone touches your painful spirit as only one sent from him could do...and there he is.

Jesus.

The man. The bronzed Galilean who spoke with such thunderous authority and loved with such childlike humility.

The God. The one who claimed to be older than time and greater than death.

Gone is the pomp of religion; dissipated is the fog of theology. Momentarily lifted is the opaque curtain of controversy and opinion. Erased are our own blinding errors and egotism. And there he stands.

Jesus.

Have you seen him?

Those who first did were never the same.

"My Lord and my God!" cried Thomas.

"I have seen the Lord," exclaimed Mary Magdalene.

"We have seen his glory," declared John.

"Were not our hearts burning within us while he talked?" rejoiced the two Emmaus-bound disciples.

But Peter said it best. "We were eyewitnesses of his majesty."

His Majesty. The emperor of Judah. The soaring eagle of eternity. The noble admiral of the Kingdom. All the splendor of heaven revealed in a human body. For a period ever so brief, the doors to the throne room were open and God came near. His Majesty was seen. Heaven touched the earth and, as a result, earth can know heaven. In astounding tandem a human body housed divinity. Holiness and earthliness intertwined.

This is no run-of-the-mill messiah. His story was extraordinary. He called himself divine, yet allowed a minimum-wage Roman soldier to drive a nail into his wrist. He demanded purity, yet stood for the rights of a repentant whore. He called men to march, yet refused to allow them to call him King. He sent men into all the world, yet equipped them with only bended knees and memories of a resurrected carpenter.

We can't regard him as simply a good teacher. His claims are too outrageous to limit him to the company of Socrates or Aristotle. Nor can we categorize him as one of many prophets sent to reveal eternal truths. His own claims eliminate that possibility.

Then who is he?

Let's try to find out. Let's follow his sandalprints. Let's sit on the cold, hard floor of the cave in which he was born. Let's smell the sawdust of the carpentry shop. Let's hear his sandals slap the hard trails of Galilee. Let's sigh as we touch the healed sores of the leper. Let's smile as we see his compassion with the woman at the well. Let's cringe as we hear the hissing of hell's Satan. Let's let our voices soar with the praises of the multitudes. Let's try to see him.

Has it been a while since you have seen him? If your prayers seem stale, it probably has. If your faith seems to be trembling, perhaps your vision of him has blurred. If you can't find power to face your problems, perhaps it is time to face him.

One warning. Something happens to a person who has witnessed His Majesty. He becomes addicted. One glimpse of the King and you are consumed by a desire to see more of him and say more about him.

Pew-warming is no longer an option. Junk religion will no longer suffice. Sensation-seeking is needless. Once you have seen his face you will forever long to see it again.

My prayer for this book—without apologies—is that the Divine Surgeon will use it as a delicate surgical tool to restore sight. That blurriness will be focused and darkness dispersed. That the Christ will emerge from a wavy figure walking out of a desert mirage to become the touchable face of a best friend. That we will lay our faces at the pierced feet and join Thomas in proclaiming, "My Lord and my God." And, most supremely, that we will whisper the secret of the universe, "We were eyewitnesses of his majesty."

PART ONE

HIS
INCARNATION

And the Word became flesh and dwelt among us,
and we beheld His glory,…full of grace and truth.

JOHN 1:14

THE ARRIVAL

How to tell the extraordinary from the ordinary?

The noise and the bustle began earlier than usual in the village. As night gave way to dawn, people were already on the streets. Vendors were positioning themselves on the corners of the most heavily traveled avenues. Store owners were unlocking the doors to their shops. Children were awakened by the excited barking of the street dogs and the complaints of donkeys pulling carts.

The owner of the inn had awakened earlier than most in the town. After all, the inn was full, all the beds taken. Every available mat or blanket had been put to use. Soon all the customers would be stirring and there would be a lot of work to do.

One's imagination is kindled thinking about the conversation of the innkeeper and his family at the breakfast table. Did anyone mention the arrival of the young couple the night before? Did anyone ask about their welfare? Did anyone comment on the pregnancy of the girl on the donkey? Perhaps. Perhaps someone raised the subject. But, at best, it was raised, not discussed. There was nothing *that* novel about them. They were, possibly, one of several families turned away that night.

Besides, who had time to talk about them when there was so much excitement in the air? Augustus did the economy of Bethlehem a favor when he decreed that a census should be taken. Who could remember when such commerce had hit the village?

No, it is doubtful that anyone mentioned the couple's arrival or wondered about the condition of the girl. They were too busy. The day was upon them. The day's bread had to be made. The morning's chores had to be done. There was too much to do to imagine that the impossible had occurred.

God had entered the world as a baby.

Yet, were someone to chance upon the sheep stable on the outskirts of Bethlehem that morning, what a peculiar scene they would behold.

The stable stinks like all stables do. The stench of urine, dung, and sheep reeks pungently in the air. The ground is hard, the hay scarce. Cobwebs cling to the ceiling and a mouse scurries across the dirt floor.

A more lowly place of birth could not exist.

Off to one side sit a group of shepherds. They sit silently on the floor; perhaps perplexed, perhaps in awe, no doubt in amazement. Their night watch had been interrupted by an explosion of light from heaven and a symphony of angels. God goes to those who have time to hear him—so on this cloudless night he went to simple shepherds.

Near the young mother sits the weary father. If anyone is dozing, he is. He can't remember the last time he sat down. And now that the excitement has subsided a bit, now that Mary and the baby are comfortable, he leans against the wall of the stable and feels his eyes grow heavy. He still hasn't figured it all out. The mystery of the event puzzles him. But he hasn't the energy to wrestle with the questions. What's important is that the baby is fine and that Mary is safe. As sleep comes he remembers the name the angel told him to use…Jesus. "We will call him Jesus."

Wide awake is Mary. My, how young she looks! Her head rests on the soft leather of Joseph's saddle. The pain has been eclipsed by wonder. She looks into the face of the baby. Her son. Her Lord. His Majesty. At this point in history, the human being who best understands who God is and what he is doing is a teenage girl in a smelly stable. She can't take her eyes off him. Somehow Mary knows she is holding God. *So this is he.* She remembers the words of the angel. "His kingdom will never end."[1]

He looks like anything but a king. His face is prunish and red. His cry, though strong and healthy, is still the helpless and piercing cry of a baby. And he is absolutely dependent upon Mary for his well-being.

Majesty in the midst of the mundane. Holiness in the filth of sheep manure and sweat. Divinity entering the world on the floor of a stable, through the womb of a teenager and in the presence of a carpenter.

She touches the face of the infant-God. *How long was your journey!* This baby had overlooked the universe. These rags keeping him warm were the robes of eternity. His golden throne room had been abandoned in favor of a dirty sheep pen. And worshiping angels had been replaced with kind but bewildered shepherds.

Meanwhile, the city hums. The merchants are unaware that God has visited their planet. The innkeeper would never believe that he had just sent God into the cold. And the people would scoff at anyone who told them the Messiah lay in the arms of a teenager on the outskirts of their village. They were all too busy to consider the possibility.

Those who missed His Majesty's arrival that night missed it not because of evil acts or malice; no, they missed it because they simply weren't looking.

Little has changed in the last two thousand years, has it?

Never when we witness something historic

CHAPTER 2

"JUST A MOMENT…"

I t all happened in a moment, a most remarkable moment.

As moments go, that one appeared no different than any other. If you could somehow pick it up off the timeline and examine it, it would look exactly like the ones that have passed while you have read these words. It came and it went. It was preceded and succeeded by others just like it. It was one of the countless moments that have marked time since eternity became measurable.

But in reality, that particular moment was like none other. For through that segment of time a spectacular thing occurred. God became a man. While the creatures of earth walked unaware, Divinity arrived. Heaven opened herself and placed her most precious one in a human womb.

The omnipotent, in one instant, made himself breakable. He who had been spirit became pierceable. He who was larger than the universe became an embryo. And he who sustains the world with a word chose to be dependent upon the nourishment of a young girl.

God as a fetus. Holiness sleeping in a womb. The creator of life being created.

God was given eyebrows, elbows, two kidneys, and a spleen. He stretched against the walls and floated in the amniotic fluids of his mother.

God had come near.

He came, not as a flash of light or as an unapproachable conqueror, but as one whose first cries were heard by a peasant girl and a sleepy carpenter. The hands that first held him were unmanicured, calloused, and dirty.

No silk. No ivory. No hype. No party. No hoopla.

Were it not for the shepherds, there would have been no reception. And were it not for a group of star-gazers, there would have been no gifts.

Angels watched as Mary changed God's diaper. The universe watched with wonder as The Almighty learned to walk. Children played in the street with him. And had the synagogue leader in Nazareth known who was listening to his sermons…

Jesus may have had pimples. He may have been tone-deaf. Perhaps a girl down the street had a crush on him or vice-versa. It could be that his knees were bony. One thing's for sure: He was, while completely divine, completely human.

For thirty-three years he would feel everything you and I have ever felt. He felt weak. He grew weary. He was afraid of failure. He was susceptible to wooing women. He got colds, burped, and had body odor. His feelings got hurt. His feet got tired. And his head ached.

To think of Jesus in such a light is—well, it seems almost irreverent, doesn't it? It's not something we like to do; it's uncomfortable. It is much easier to keep the humanity out of the incarnation. Clean the manure from around the manger. Wipe the sweat out of his eyes. Pretend he never snored or blew his nose or hit his thumb with a hammer.

He's easier to stomach that way. There is something about keeping him divine that keeps him distant, packaged, predictable.

But don't do it. For heaven's sake, don't. Let him be as human as he intended to be. Let him into the mire and muck of our world. For only if we let him in can he pull us out.

Listen to him.

"Love your neighbor" was spoken by a man whose neighbors tried to kill him.[1]

The challenge to leave family for the gospel was issued by one who kissed his mother good-bye in the doorway.[2]

"Pray for those who persecute you" came from the lips that would soon be begging God to forgive his murderers.[3]

"I am with you always" are the words of a God who in one instant did the impossible to make it all possible for you and me.[4]

It all happened in a moment. In one moment…a most remarkable moment. The Word became flesh.

There will be another. The world will see another instantaneous transformation. You see, in becoming man, God made it possible for man to see God. When Jesus went home he left the back door open. As a result, "we will all be changed—in a moment, in the twinkling of an eye."[5]

The first moment of transformation went unnoticed by the world. But you can bet your sweet September that the second one won't. The next time you use the phrase "just a moment,…" remember that's all the time it will take to change this world.

CHAPTER 3

ABSURDITY IN THE FLESH

Y*ou mean to tell me God became a baby…"*
The one posing the questions was puzzled. His thick eyebrows furrowed in doubt and his eyes squinted in caution. Though there were places to sit, he opted not to do so. He preferred to stand safely behind the crowd, unsure, yet intrigued by what he was hearing. Throughout the lecture he had listened intently, occasionally uncrossing his arms to stroke his whiskered chin. Now, however, he stood upright, punching the air with his finger as he queried.

"and that he was born in a sheep stable?"

He looked as though he'd walked down from one of the adjacent Colorado mountains: stocking hat, down vest, nylon leggings, hiking boots. And he sounded as though he honestly didn't know if the story he was hearing was a mountain legend or the gospel truth.

"Yes, that is what I mean to say," the lecturer responded.

"And then, after becoming a baby, he was raised in a blue-collar home? He never wrote any books or held any offices, yet he called himself the Son of God?"

"That is right."

The lecturer being questioned was Landon Saunders; the voice of the Heartbeat Radio program. I've never heard anybody tell the story of the Nazarene like Landon can.

"He never traveled outside of his own country, never studied at a university, never lived in a palace, and yet asked to be regarded as the creator of the universe?"

"That's correct."

I was a bit unnerved by the dialogue. I was fresh out of college, gung ho, enthusiastic. As a volunteer helper in the lecture series, I had come with memorized verses and responses loaded in the chamber of my evangelistic six-shooter. However, I came prepared to defend a lifestyle, not a Savior. I was ready to argue morality, doctrine, heaven and hell. I wasn't ready to argue a man. Jesus had always been someone I just accepted. These questions were a bit too aggressive for my virgin faith.

"And this crucifixion story…he was betrayed by his own people? No followers came to his defense? And then he was executed like a common junkyard thief?"

"That's the gist of it."

The authenticity of the questioner didn't allow you to regard him as a cynic nor to dismiss him as a show-off. To the contrary, he seemed nervous about commanding such attention. His awkwardness betrayed his inexperience in public speaking. But his desire to know was just an ounce or two heavier than his discomfort, so he continued.

"And after the killing he was buried in a borrowed grave?"

"Yes, he had no grave of his own, nor money with which to purchase one."

The honesty of the dialogue kept the audience spellbound. I realized I was witnessing one of those rare times when two people were willing to question the holy. Here were two men standing on opposite sides of a deep chasm, one asking the other if the bridge that stretched between them could actually be trusted.

There was a hint of emotion in the student's voice as he carefully worded the next question.

"And according to what's written, after three days in the grave he was resurrected and made appearances to over five hundred people?"

"Yes."

"And all this was to prove that God still loves his people and provides a way for us to return to him?"

"Right."

I knew which question was coming next. Every one in the room knew it. It could have gone without being asked. In my heart of hearts, I was hoping that it wouldn't be asked.

"Doesn't that all sound rather..." He paused a second, searching for the right adjective. *"Doesn't that all sound rather absurd?"*

All the heads turned in perfect sync and looked at Landon. All the heads, that is, except mine. My head was spinning as I was forced to look at Jesus from a new angle. Christianity...absurd? Jesus on a cross...absurd? The Incarnation...absurd? The Resurrection...absurd? My Sunday school Jesus had been taken down from the flannel board.

Landon's response was simple. *"Yes. Yes, I suppose it does sound absurd, doesn't it?"*

I didn't like that answer. I didn't like it at all. Tell the fellow how it made sense! Diagram the dispensations. Present fulfilled prophecies. Explain the fulfillment of the Old Law. Covenant. Reconciliation. Redemption. Sure it made sense. Don't let him describe God's actions as absurd!

Then it began to dawn on me: *What* God did makes sense. It makes sense that Jesus would be our sacrifice because a sacrifice was needed to justify man's presence before God. It makes sense that God would use the Old Law to tutor Israel on their need for grace. It makes sense that Jesus would be our High Priest. *What* God did makes sense. It can be taught, charted, and put in books on systematic theology.

However, *why* God did it is absolutely absurd. When one leaves the method and examines the motive, the carefully stacked blocks of logic begin to tumble. That type of love isn't logical; it can't be neatly outlined in a sermon or explained in a term paper.

Think about it. For thousands of years, using his wit and charm, man had tried to be friends with God. And for thousands of years he had let God down more than he had lifted him up. He'd done the very thing he promised he'd never do. It was a fiasco. Even the holiest of the heroes sometimes forgot whose side they were on. Some of the scenarios in the Bible look more like the adventures of Sinbad the Sailor than stories for vacation Bible school. Remember these characters?

Aaron. Right-hand man to Moses. Witness of the plagues. Member of the "Red Sea Riverbed Expedition." Holy priest of God. But if he was so saintly, what is he doing leading the Israelites in fireside aerobics in front of the golden calf?

The sons of Jacob. The fathers of the tribes of Israel. Great-grandsons of Abraham. Yet, if they were so special, why were they gagging their younger brother and sending him to Egypt?

David. The man after God's own heart. The King's king. The giant-slayer and songwriter. He's also the guy whose glasses got steamy as a result of a bath on a roof. Unfortunately, the water wasn't his, nor was the woman he was watching.

And Samson. Swooning on Delilah's couch, drunk on the wine, perfume, and soft lights. He's thinking, *She's putting on something more comfortable.* She's thinking, *I know I put those shears in here somewhere.*

Adam adorned in fig leaves and stains of forbidden fruit. Moses throwing both a staff and a temper tantrum. King Saul looking into a crystal ball for the will of God. Noah, drunk and naked in his own tent.

These are the chosen ones of God? This is the royal lineage of the King? These are the ones who were to carry out God's mission?

It's easy to see the absurdity.

Why didn't he give up? Why didn't he let the globe spin off its axis?

Even after generations of people had spit in his face, he still loved them. After a nation of chosen ones had stripped him naked and ripped his incarnated flesh, he still died for them. And even today, after billions have chosen to prostitute themselves before the pimps of power, fame, and wealth, he still waits for them.

It *is* inexplicable. It doesn't have a drop of logic nor a thread of rationality.

And yet, it is that very irrationality that gives the gospel its greatest defense. For only God could love like that.

I don't know what happened to that inquisitive fellow in Colorado. He disappeared as quickly as he came. But I'm in his debt. He forced me to see Jesus as I'd never seen him.

At first I didn't recognize him. I guess I was expecting someone in a flowing frock with silky-white hands. But it was he. The lion. The Judean Lion. He walked out from among the dense trees of theology and ritual and lay down in a brief clearing. In his paw was a wound and in his mane were stains of blood. But there was a royalty about him that silenced even the breeze in the trees.

Bloodstained royalty. A God with tears. A creator with a heart. God became earth's mockery to save his children.

How absurd to think that such nobility would go to such poverty to share such a treasure with such thankless souls.

But he did.

In fact, the only thing more absurd than the gift is our stubborn unwillingness to receive it.

CHAPTER 4

MARY'S PRAYER

G od. O infant-God. Heaven's fairest child. Conceived by the union of divine grace with our disgrace. Sleep well.

Sleep well. Bask in the coolness of this night bright with diamonds. Sleep well, for the heat of anger simmers nearby. Enjoy the silence of the crib, for the noise of confusion rumbles in your future. Savor the sweet safety of my arms, for a day is soon coming when I cannot protect you.

Rest well, tiny hands. For though you belong to a king, you will touch no satin, own no gold. You will grasp no pen, guide no brush. No, your tiny hands are reserved for works more precious:

to touch a lepers open wound,
to wipe a widow's weary tear,
to claw the ground of Gethsemane.

Your hands, so tiny, so tender, so white—clutched tonight in an infant's fist. They aren't destined to hold a scepter nor wave from a palace balcony. They are reserved instead for a Roman spike that will staple them to a Roman cross.

Sleep deeply, tiny eyes. Sleep while you can. For soon the blurriness will clear and you will see the mess we have made of your world.

You will see our nakedness, for we cannot hide.

You will see our selfishness, for we cannot give.
You will see our pain, for we cannot heal.

O eyes that will see hell's darkest pit and witness her ugly prince…sleep, please sleep; sleep while you can.

Lay still, tiny mouth. Lay still mouth from which eternity will speak.
   Tiny tongue that will soon summon the dead,

      that will define grace,
      that will silence our foolishness.

Rosebud lips—upon which ride a starborn kiss of forgiveness to those who believe you, and of death to those who deny you—lay still.

And tiny feet cupped in the palm of my hand, rest. For many difficult steps lie ahead for you.

   Do you taste the dust of the trails you will travel?
   Do you feel the cold sea water upon which you will walk?
   Do you wrench at the invasion of the nail you will bear?
   Do you fear the steep descent down the spiral staircase into Satan's domain?

   Rest, tiny feet. Rest today so that tomorrow you might walk with power. Rest. For millions will follow in your steps.

And little heart…holy…pumping the blood of life through the universe: How many times will we break you?

   You'll be torn by the thorns of our accusations.
   You'll be ravaged by the cancer of our sin.
   You'll be crushed under the weight of your own sorrow.
   And you'll be pierced by the spear of our rejection.

Yet in that piercing, in that ultimate ripping of muscle and membrane, in that final rush of blood and water, you will find rest. Your hands will be freed, your eyes will see justice, your lips will smile, and your feet will carry you home.

And there you'll rest again—this time in the embrace of your Father.

CHAPTER 5

LIMB-CLIMBER OR BRANCH-SITTER

Joseph was perched firmly on his branch in the tree. It was thick, reliable, and perfect for sitting. It was so strong that he didn't tremble when the storms came, nor did he shake when the winds blew. No, this branch was predictable and solid and Joseph had no intention of leaving it.

That is, until he was told to go out on a limb.

As he sat securely on his branch, he looked up at the limb God wanted him to climb. He'd never seen one so thin! "That's no place for a man to go!" he said to himself. "There's no place to sit. There's no protection from the weather. And how could you sleep dangling from that quivering twig?" He inched back a bit, leaned against the trunk, and pondered the situation.

Common sense told him not to go out on the limb. "Conceived by the Holy Spirit? Come on!"

Self-defense told him not to do it. "Who will believe me? What will our families think?"

Convenience told him not to do it. "Just when I was hoping to settle down and raise a family."

Pride told him not to do it. "If she expects me to buy a tale like that…"

But God had told him to do it. And that's what bothered him.

It bothered him because he was happy where he was. Life next to the trunk was good. His branch was big enough to allow him to sit in comfort. He was near scores of other branch-sitters and had made some valid contributions to the tree community. After all, didn't he make regular vis-its to the sick at the North Branch Medical Center? And wasn't he the best tenor in the Treedom Singers Chorale? And what about the class he taught on religious heritage, appropriately entitled "Our Family Tree"? Surely God wouldn't want him to leave. He had…well, you could say that he had roots here.

Besides, he knew the kind of fellow who goes out on a limb. Radical. Extremist. Liberal. Always going overboard. Always stirring the leaves. Guys with their heads full of strange ideas in search of foreign fruit. Why, the stable ones are the ones who know how to stay close to home and leave well enough alone.

I have a feeling some of you can relate to Joseph. You know how he feels, don't you? You've been there. You're smiling because you, too, have been called to go out on a limb a time or two. You know the imbalance that comes from having one foot in your will and one foot in his. You, too, have sunk your fingernails into the bark to get a better grip. You know too well the butterflies that swarm in the pit of your stomach when you realize changes are in the air.

Perhaps changes are in the air right now. Maybe you're in the midst of a decision. It's disrupting, isn't it? You like your branch. You've grown accustomed to it and it to you. And, like Joseph, you've been a pretty good branch-sitter. And then you hear the call. "I need you to go out on the limb and

> …take a stand. Some of the local churches are organizing an anti-pornography campaign. They need some volunteers."

> …move. Take your family and move overseas; I have a special work for you."

> …forgive. It doesn't matter who hurt who first. What matters is that you go and build the bridge."

> …evangelize. That new family down the block? They don't know anyone in town. Go meet them."

…sacrifice. The orphanage has a mortgage payment due this month. They can't meet it. Remember the bonus you received last week?"

Regardless of the nature of the call, the consequences are the same: civil war. Though your heart may say yes, your feet say no. Excuses blow as numerously as golden leaves in an autumn wind. "That's not my talent." "It's time for someone else to take charge." "Not now. I'll get to it tomorrow."

But eventually you're left staring at a bare tree and a hard choice: His will or yours?

Joseph chose his. After all, it was really the only option. Joseph knew *to* that the only thing worse than a venture into the unknown was the *know* thought of denying his Master. So, resolute, he grasped the smaller limb. *it is* With tight lips and a determined glint in his eye, he placed one hand in front of the other until he dangled in the air with only his faith in God *the* as a safety net. *Master*

As things turned out, Joseph's fears were justified. Life wasn't as comfortable as it had been. The limb he grasped was, indeed, a slender one: The Messiah was to be born to Mary and to be raised in his home. He took cold showers for nine months so the baby could be born of a virgin. He had to push away the sheep and clear out the cow patties so his wife would have a place to give birth. He became a fugitive of the law. He spent two years trying to understand Egyptian.

At times that limb must have bounced furiously in the wind. But Joseph just shut his eyes and held on. But you can be sure of one thing. He never regretted it. Sweet was the reward for his courage. One look in the face of that heavenly toddler and he knew he would do it again in a heartbeat.

Have you been called to go out on a limb for God? You can bet it won't be easy. Limb-climbing has never been easy. Ask Joseph. Or, better yet, ask Jesus.

He knows better than anyone the cost of hanging on a tree.

CHAPTER 6

TWENTY-FIVE QUESTIONS FOR MARY

What was it like watching him pray?

How did he respond when he saw other kids giggling during the service at the synagogue?

When he saw a rainbow, did he ever mention a flood?

Did you ever feel awkward teaching him how he created the world?

When he saw a lamb being led to the slaughter, did he act differently?

Did you ever see him with a distant look on his face as if he were listening to someone you couldn't hear?

How did he act at funerals?

Did the thought ever occur to you that the God to whom you were praying was asleep under your own roof?

Did you ever try to count the stars with him…and succeed?

Did he ever come home with a black eye?

How did he act when he got his first haircut?

Did he have any friends by the name of Judas?

Did he do well in school?

Did you ever scold him?

Did he ever have to ask a question about Scripture?

What do you think he thought when he saw a prostitute offering to the highest bidder the body he made?

Did he ever get angry when someone was dishonest with him?

Did you ever catch him pensively looking at the flesh on his own arm while holding a clod of dirt?

Did he ever wake up afraid?

Who was his best friend?

When someone referred to Satan, how did he act?
Did you ever accidentally call him Father?
What did he and his cousin John talk about as kids?
Did his other brothers and sisters understand what was happening?
Did you ever think, *That's God eating my soup?*

CHAPTER 7

CHRISTMAS NIGHT

It's Christmas night. The house is quiet. Even the crackle is gone from the fireplace. Warm coals issue a lighthouse glow in the darkened den. Stockings hang empty on the mantle. The tree stands naked in the corner. Christmas cards, tinsel, and memories remind Christmas night of Christmas Day.

It's Christmas night. What a day it has been! Spiced tea. Santa Claus. Cranberry sauce. "Thank you so much." "You shouldn't have!" "Grandma is on the phone." Knee-deep wrapping paper. "It just fits." Flashing cameras.

It's Christmas night. The girls are in bed. Jenna dreams of her talking Big Bird and clutches her new purse. Andrea sleeps in her new Santa pajamas.

It's Christmas night. The tree that only yesterday grew from soil made of gifts, again grows from the Christmas tree stand. Presents are now possessions. Wrapping paper is bagged and in the dumpster. The dishes are washed and leftover turkey awaits next week's sandwiches.

It's Christmas night. The last of the carolers appeared on the ten o'clock news. The last of the apple pie was eaten by my brother-in-law. And the last of the Christmas albums have been stored away having dutifully performed their annual rendition of chestnuts, white Christmases, and red-nosed reindeers.

It's Christmas night.

The midnight hour has chimed and I should be asleep, but I'm awake. I'm kept awake by one stunning thought. The world was different this week. It was temporarily transformed.

Did we (handwritten margin note)

The magical dust of Christmas glittered on the cheeks of humanity ever so briefly, reminding us of what is worth having and what we were intended to be. We forgot our compulsion with winning, wooing, and warring. We put away our ladders and ledgers, we hung up our stopwatches and weapons. We stepped off our race tracks and roller coasters and looked outward toward the star of Bethlehem.

It's the season to be jolly because, more than at any other time, we think of him. More than in any other season, his name is on our lips.

And the result? For a few precious hours our heavenly yearnings intermesh and we become a chorus. A ragtag chorus of longshoremen, Boston lawyers, illegal immigrants, housewives, and a thousand other peculiar persons who are banking that Bethlehem's mystery is in reality, a reality. "Come and behold him" we sing, stirring even the sleepiest of shepherds and pointing them toward the Christ-child.

Do they? (handwritten margin note)

For a few precious hours, he is beheld. Christ the Lord. Those who pass the year without seeing him, suddenly see him. People who have been accustomed to using his name in vain, pause to use it in praise. Eyes, now free of the blinders of self, marvel at his majesty.

All of a sudden he's everywhere.

In the grin of the policeman as he drives the paddy wagon full of presents to the orphanage.

In the twinkle in the eyes of the Taiwanese waiter as he tells of his upcoming Christmas trip to see his children.

In the emotion of the father who is too thankful to finish the dinner table prayer.

He's in the tears of the mother as she welcomes home her son from overseas.

He's in the heart of the man who spent Christmas morning on skid row giving away cold baloney sandwiches and warm wishes.

And he's in the solemn silence of the crowd of shopping mall shoppers as the elementary school chorus sings "Away in a Manger."

Emmanuel. He is with us. God came near.

It's Christmas night. In a few hours the cleanup will begin—lights will come down, trees will be thrown out. Size 36 will be exchanged for size 40, eggnog will be on sale for half price. Soon life will be normal again. December's generosity will become January's payments and the magic will begin to fade.

But for the moment, the magic is still in the air. Maybe that's why I'm still awake. I want to savor the spirit just a bit more. I want to pray that those who beheld him today will look for him next August. And I can't help but linger on one fanciful thought: If he can do so much with such timid prayers lamely offered in December, how much more could he do if we thought of him every day?

CHAPTER 8

OUT OF THE
CARPENTRY SHOP

The heavy door creaked on its hinges as he pushed it open. With a few strides he crossed the silent shop and opened the wooden shutters to a square shaft of sunshine that pierced the darkness, painting a box of daylight on the dirt floor.

He looked around the carpentry shop. He stood a moment in the refuge of the little room that housed so many sweet memories. He balanced the hammer in his hand. He ran his fingers across the sharp teeth of the saw. He stroked the smoothly worn wood of the sawhorse. He had come to say good-bye.

It was time for him to leave. He had heard something that made him know it was time to go. So he came one last time to smell the sawdust and lumber.

Life was peaceful here. Life was so…safe.

Here he had spent countless hours of contentment. On this dirt floor he had played as a toddler while his father worked. Here Joseph had taught him how to grip a hammer. And on this workbench he had built his first chair.

I wonder what he thought as he took one last look around the room. Perhaps he stood for a moment at the workbench looking at the tiny shadows cast by the chisel and shavings. Perhaps he listened as voices from the past filled the air.

"Good job, Jesus."

"Joseph, Jesus—come and eat!"

"Don't worry, sir, we'll get it finished on time. I'll get Jesus to help me."

I wonder if he hesitated. I wonder if his heart was torn. I wonder if he rolled a nail between his thumb and fingers, anticipating the pain.

It was in the carpentry shop that he must have given birth to his thoughts. Here concepts and convictions were woven together to form the fabric of his ministry.

You can almost see the tools of the trade in his words as he spoke. You can see the trueness of a plumb line as he called for moral standards. You can hear the whistle of the plane as he pleads for religion to shave away unnecessary traditions. You can picture the snugness of a dovetail as he demands loyalty in relationships. You can imagine him with a pencil and a ledger as he urges honesty.

It was here that his human hands shaped the wood his divine hands had created. And it was here that his body matured while his spirit waited for the right moment, the right day.

And now that day had arrived.

It must have been difficult to leave. After all, life as a carpenter wasn't bad. It wasn't bad at all. Business was good. The future was bright and his work was enjoyable.

In Nazareth he was known only as Jesus, the son of Joseph. You can be sure he was respected in the community. He was good with his hands. He had many friends. He was a favorite among the children. He could tell a good joke and had a habit of filling the air with contagious laughter.

I wonder if he wanted to stay. "I could do a good job here in Nazareth. Settle down. Raise a family. Be a civic leader."

I wonder because I know he had already read the last chapter. He knew that the feet that would step out of the safe shadow of the carpentry shop would not rest until they'd been pierced and placed on a Roman cross.

You see, he didn't have to go. He had a choice. He could have stayed. He could have kept his mouth shut. He could have ignored the call or at least postponed it. And had he chosen to stay, who would've known? Who would have blamed him?

He could have come back as a man in another era when society wasn't so volatile, when religion wasn't so stale, when people would listen better.

He could have come back when crosses were out of style.

But his heart wouldn't let him. If there was hesitation on the part of his humanity, it was overcome by the compassion of his divinity. His divinity heard the voices. His divinity heard the hopeless cries of the poor, the bitter accusations of the abandoned, the dangling despair of those who are trying to save themselves.

And his divinity saw the faces. Some wrinkled. Some weeping. Some hidden behind veils. Some obscured by fear. Some earnest with searching. Some blank with boredom. From the face of Adam to the face of the infant born somewhere in the world as you read these words, he saw them all.

And you can be sure of one thing. Among the voices that found their way into that carpentry shop in Nazareth was your voice. Your silent prayers uttered on tearstained pillows were heard before they were said. Your deepest questions about death and eternity were answered before they were asked. And your direst need, your need for a Savior, was met before you ever sinned.

And not only did he hear you, he saw you. He saw your face aglow the hour you first knew him. He saw your face in shame the hour you first fell. The same face that looked back at you from this morning's mirror, looked at him. And it was enough to kill him.

He left because of you.

He laid his security down with his hammer. He hung tranquillity on the peg with his nail apron. He closed the window shutters on the sunshine of his youth and locked the door on the comfort and ease of anonymity.

Since he could bear your sins more easily than he could bear the thought of your hopelessness, he chose to leave.

It wasn't easy. Leaving the carpentry shop never has been.

CHAPTER 9

"JUST CALL ME JESUS"

Many of the names in the Bible that refer to our Lord are nothing less than palatial and august: Son of God, The Lamb of God, The Light of the World, The Resurrection and the Life, The Bright and Morning Star, He that Should Come, Alpha and Omega.

They are phrases that stretch the boundaries of human language in an effort to capture the uncapturable, the grandeur of God. And try as they might to draw as near as they may, they always fall short. Hearing them is somewhat like hearing a Salvation Army Christmas band on the street corner play Handel's *Messiah*. Good try, but it doesn't work. The message is too majestic for the medium.

And such it is with language. The phrase "There are no words to express…" is really the only one that can honestly be applied to God. No names do him justice.

But there is one name which recalls a quality of the Master that bewildered and compelled those who knew him. It reveals a side of him that, when recognized, is enough to make you fall on your face.

It is not too small, nor is it too grand. It is a name that fits like the shoe fit Cinderella's foot.

Jesus.

In the gospels it's his most common name—used almost six hundred times. And a common name it was. Jesus is the Greek form of Joshua, Jeshua, and Jehoshua—all familiar Old Testament names. There were at least five high priests known as Jesus. The writings of the historian Josephus refer to about twenty people called Jesus. The New Testament speaks of Jesus Justus, the friend of Paul,[1] and the sorcerer of Paphos is called Bar-Jesus.[2] Some manuscripts give Jesus as the first name of Barabbas. "Which would you like me to release to you—Jesus Barabbas or Jesus called the Messiah?"[3]

What's the point? Jesus could have been a "Joe." If Jesus came today, his name might have been John or Bob or Jim. Were he here today, it is doubtful he would distance himself with a lofty name like Reverend Holiness Angelic Divinity III. No, when God chose the name his son would carry, he chose a human name.[4] He chose a name so typical that it would appear two or three times on any given class roll.

"The Word became flesh," John said, in other words.

He was touchable, approachable, reachable. And, what's more, he was ordinary. If he were here today you probably wouldn't notice him as he walked through a shopping mall. He wouldn't turn heads by the clothes he wore or the jewelry he flashed.

"Just call me Jesus," you can almost hear him say.

He was the kind of fellow you'd invite to watch the Rams-Giants game at your house. He'd wrestle on the floor with your kids, doze on your couch, and cook steaks on your grill. He'd laugh at your jokes and tell a few of his own. And when you spoke, he'd listen to you as if he had all the time in eternity.

And one thing's for sure, you'd invite him back.

It is worth noting that those who knew him best remembered him as Jesus. The titles Jesus Christ and Lord Jesus are seen only six times. Those who walked with him remembered him not with a title or designation, but with a name—Jesus.

Think about the implications. When God chose to reveal himself to mankind, what medium did he use? A book? No, that was secondary. A church? No. That was consequential. A moral code? No. To limit God's revelation to a cold list of do's and don'ts is as tragic as looking at a Colorado road map and saying that you'd seen the Rockies.

When God chose to reveal himself, he did so (surprise of surprises) through a human body. The tongue that called forth the dead was a human one. The hand that touched the leper had dirt under its nails. The feet upon which the woman wept were calloused and dusty. And his tears…oh, don't miss the tears…they came from a heart as broken as yours or mine ever has been.

"For we do not have a high priest who is unable to sympathize with our weaknesses."[5]

So, people came to him. My, how they came to him! They came at night; they touched him as he walked down the street; they followed him around the sea; they invited him into their homes and placed their children at his feet. Why? Because he refused to be a statue in a cathedral or a priest in an elevated pulpit. He chose instead to be Jesus.

There is not a hint of one person who was afraid to draw near him. There were those who mocked him. There were those who were envious of him. There were those who misunderstood him. There were those who revered him. But there was not one person who considered him too holy, too divine, or too celestial to touch. *There was not one person who was reluctant to approach him for fear of being rejected.*

Remember that.

Remember that the next time you find yourself amazed at your own failures.

Or the next time acidic accusations burn holes in your soul.

Or the next time you see a cold cathedral or hear a lifeless liturgy.

Remember. It is man who creates the distance. It is Jesus who builds the bridge.

"Just call me Jesus."

CHAPTER 10

WOMEN OF WINTER

I

The mourners didn't cause him to stop. Nor did the large crowd, or even the body of the dead man on the stretcher. It was the woman—the look on her face and the redness in her eyes. He knew immediately what was happening. It was her son who was being carried out, her only son. And if anyone knows the pain that comes from losing your only son, God does.

So he did it; he went into action. "Don't cry" he told the mother. "Arise!" he told the boy. The dead man spoke, the devil ran, and the people were reminded of this truth: For those who know the Author of Life, death is nothing more than Satan's dead-man's-bluff.[1]

II

His plan was to catch a few winks while the boys went to town for food. And what better place to rest than a well at noon. No one comes for water at this hour. So he sat down, stretched his arms, and leaned against the wall of the well. But his nap was soon interrupted. He opened one eye just wide enough to see her trudging up the trail with a heavy jar on her shoulder. Behind her came half a dozen kids, each one looking like a different daddy.

She didn't have to say a word. Her life story was written in the wrinkles on her face. The wounds of five broken romances were gaping and festered. Each man who had left her had taken a piece of her heart. Now she wasn't sure there was anything left.

"And the man you now live with won't even give you his name." Jesus said it for her. He understood her pain too well. Far more than five men had broken commitments to him.

Silently the Divine Surgeon reached into his kit and pulled out a needle of faith and a thread of hope. In the shade of Jacob's well he stitched her wounded soul back together. "There will come a day…" he whispered.[2]

III

By the time she got to Jesus, she had nothing left. The doctors had taken her last dime. The diagnosis had stolen her last hope. And the hemorrhage had robbed her of her last drop of energy. She had no more money, no more friends, and no more options. With the end of her rope in one hand and a wing and a prayer in her heart, she shoved her way through the crowd.

When her hand touched his garment a transfusion occurred. He let it go out and she let it go in.

It didn't bother Jesus that the woman came to him as a last resort. To him it mattered only that she came. He knows that with some of us it takes a lot of reality to snap us to our senses, so he doesn't keep a time clock. Those who scramble in at quitting time get the same wage as those who beat the morning whistle. I guess that's what makes grace, grace.[3]

Three women. One bereaved. One rejected. One dying. All alone.

Alone in the winter of life.

Though we don't know what they looked like, it would be fair to assume they had passed the peak of their desirability. The only heads that turned as they walked down the street were heads shaking with pity. One of the three was widowed and childless; another had lost her innocence six bedrooms back; and the third was broke, desperate, and dying.

Had Jesus ignored them, who would have noticed? In a culture where women were only a grade or two above farm animals no one would've thought any less had he walked silently past the funeral or closed his eyes and leaned back against the well or ignored the tug on his robe. After all, they were only women!

Worn,
   wrinkled,
      weary women.
         Winter women.

Let them alone, Jesus, one could reason. Find someone with a bit of springtime about them.

By the world's standards these three could give nothing in return. They'd served their purpose: borne their children, fed their families, pleased their men. Now it was time to push them out into the cold until they died, making room for the young and spotless.

That's where Jesus found them. Shivering in the icy sleet of uselessness.

The raw winter of life.

Sound familiar? Sure it does. We have our own people of winter. People who for the lack of good looks or sufficient earning power wander around like porcupines at a picnic, unwanted and unapproachable.

Hard to believe?

Visit a high school sometime and look for the teenagers already feeling the chilly winds of rejection. They are easy to find. They're the ones with acne, or greasy hair, or holes in their shoes; they sit alone at lunch and stay at home on weekends. They orbit around the class stars, longing for acceptance yet increasingly convinced they don't deserve it.

Or try Miami Beach. I don't mean the north beach where tourists pay $150 a day to get sunburned. I mean the south beach, a city deliberately built for the exhausted. Watch them shuffle aged feet down the sidewalk. They have come to their burial ground. They have fulfilled their function and now fill their days with dominoes, dogs, and doctor visits. They fill their nights with dreams of the granddaughter who might come next Christmas. And though the Gold Coast is warm, in their souls blow the winds of winter.

Or consider the unborn. Every twenty seconds one is taken from the warmth of the womb and cast into the cold lake of selfishness. In spite of the clinical phrases used to make the act more palatable—"termination of pregnancy" rather than "abortion," "fetus" instead of "unborn child," "conceptus" as opposed to "baby"—the act is deplorable. The bottom line is still a denial of the inherent value of a human being.

The paragraphs could go on and on. Paragraphs about quadriplegics, AIDS victims, or the terminally ill. Single parents. Alcoholics. Divorcées. The blind. All are social outcasts. Lepers, mutations. All, to one degree or another, shunned by the "normal world."

Society doesn't know what to do with them. And, sadly, even the Church doesn't know what to do with them. They often would find a warmer reception at the corner bar than in a Sunday school class.

But Jesus would find a place for them. He would find a place for them because he cares. And he cares unconditionally.

No, no one would have blamed Jesus for ignoring the three women. To have turned his head would have been much easier, less controversial, and not nearly as risky. But God, who made them, couldn't do that. And we, who follow him, can't either.

WHEN GOD SIGHED

wo days ago I read a word in the Bible that has since taken up
residence in my heart.

To be honest, I didn't quite know what to do with it. It's only
one word, and not a very big one at that. When I ran across the word,
(which, by the way, is exactly what happened; I was running through the
passage and this word came out of nowhere and bounced me like a speed
bump) I didn't know what to do with it. I didn't have any hook to hang
it on or category to file it under.

It was an enigmatic word in an enigmatic passage. But now, forty-
eight hours later, I have found a place for it, a place all its own. My, what
a word it is. Don't read it unless you don't mind changing your mind,
because this little word might move your spiritual furniture around a bit.

Look at the passage with me.

Then Jesus left the vicinity of Tyre and went through Sidon,
down to the Sea of Galilee and into the region of the Decapolis.
There some people brought a man to him who was deaf and
could hardly talk, and they begged him to place his hand on the
man.

After he took him aside, away from the crowd, Jesus put his
fingers into the man's ears. Then he spit and touched the man's
tongue. He looked up to heaven and with a deep sigh said to
him, *"Ephphatha!"* (which means, "Be opened!"). At this, the
man's ears were opened, his tongue was loosened and he began
to speak plainly.[1]

Quite a passage, isn't it?

Jesus is presented with a man who is deaf and has a speech impediment. Perhaps he stammered. Maybe he spoke with a lisp. Perhaps, because of his deafness, he never learned to articulate words properly.

Jesus, refusing to exploit the situation, took the man aside. He looked him in the face. Knowing it would be useless to talk, he explained what he was about to do through gestures. He spat and touched the man's tongue, telling him that whatever restricted his speech was about to be removed. He touched his ears. They, for the first time, were about to hear.

But before the man said a word or heard a sound, Jesus did something I never would have anticipated.

He sighed.

I might have expected a clap or a song or a prayer. Even a "Hallelujah!" or a brief lesson might have been appropriate. But the Son of God did none of these. Instead, he paused, looked into heaven, and sighed. From the depths of his being came a rush of emotion that said more than words.

Sigh. The word seemed out of place.

I'd never thought of God as one who sighs. I'd thought of God as one who commands. I'd thought of God as one who weeps. I'd thought of God as one who called forth the dead with a command or created the universe with a word…but a God who sighs?

Perhaps this phrase caught my eye because I do my share of sighing.

I sighed yesterday when I visited a lady whose invalid husband had deteriorated so much he didn't recognize me. He thought I was trying to sell him something.

I sighed when the dirty-faced, scantily dressed, six-year-old girl in the grocery store asked me for some change.

And I sighed today listening to a husband tell how his wife won't forgive him.

No doubt you've done your share of sighing.

If you have teenagers, you've probably sighed. If you've tried to resist temptation, you've probably sighed. If you've had your motives questioned or your best acts of love rejected, you have been forced to take a deep breath and let escape a painful sigh.

I realize there exists a sigh of relief, a sigh of expectancy, and even a sigh of joy. But that isn't the sigh described in Mark 7. The sigh described is a hybrid of frustration and sadness. It lies somewhere between a fit of anger and a burst of tears.

The apostle Paul spoke of this sighing. Twice he said that Christians will sigh as long as we are on earth and long for heaven. The creation sighs as if she were giving birth. Even the Spirit sighs as he interprets our prayers.[2]

All these sighs come from the same anxiety; a recognition of pain that was never intended, or of hope deferred.

Man was not created to be separated from his creator; hence he sighs, longing for home. The creation was never intended to be inhabited by evil; hence she sighs, yearning for the Garden. And conversations with God were never intended to depend on a translator; hence the Spirit groans on our behalf, looking to a day when humans will see God face to face.

And when Jesus looked into the eyes of Satan's victim, the only appropriate thing to do was sigh. "It was never intended to be this way," the sigh said. "Your ears weren't made to be deaf, your tongue wasn't made to stumble." The imbalance of it all caused the Master to languish.

So, I found a place for the word. You might think it strange, but I placed it beside the word *comfort,* for in an indirect way, God's pain is our comfort.

And in the agony of Jesus lies our hope. Had he not sighed, had he not felt the burden for what was not intended, we would be in a pitiful condition. Had he simply chalked it all up to the inevitable or washed his hands of the whole stinking mess, what hope would we have?

But he didn't. That holy sigh assures us that God still groans for his people. He groans for the day when all sighs will cease, when what was intended to be will be.

CHAPTER 12

THE QUESTION FOR THE CANYON'S EDGE

H*ow was the night?"* asked the nurse.

The young man's weary eyes answered the question before his lips could. It had been long and hard. Vigils always are. But even more so when they are with your own father.

"He didn't wake up."

The son sat by the bed and held the bony hand that had so often held his own. He was afraid to release it for fear that doing so might allow the man he so dearly loved to tumble over the brink. He had held it all night as the two stood on the canyon's edge, aware of the final step that was only hours away.

With words painted black with confusion, he summarized the fears that had been his companions during the darkness. "I know it has to happen," the son yearned, looking at his father's ashen face; "I just don't know why."

The canyon of death.

It is a desolate canyon. The dry ground is cracked and lifeless. A blistering sun heats the wind that moans eerily and stings mercilessly. Tears burn and words come slowly as visitors to the canyon are forced to stare into the ravine. The bottom of the crevice is invisible, the other side unreachable. You can't help but wonder what is hidden in the darkness. And you can't help but long to leave.

Have you been there? Have you been called to stand at the thin line that separates the living from the dead? Have you lain awake at night listening to machines pumping air in and out of your lungs? Have you watched sickness corrode and atrophy the body of a friend? Have you lingered behind at the cemetery long after the others have left, gazing in disbelief at the metal casket that contains the body that contained the soul of the one you can't believe is gone?

If so, then this canyon is not unfamiliar to you. You've heard the lonesome whistle of the winds. You've heard the painful questions Why? What for? ricochet answerless off the canyon walls. And you've kicked loose rocks off the edge and listened for the sound of their crashing, which never comes.

The young father crushed the cigarette into the plastic ashtray. He was alone in the hospital waiting room. How long will it take? It all had happened so quickly! First came the news from the hospital, then the frantic drive to the emergency room and then the explanation of the nurse. "Your son was hit by a car. He has some serious head wounds. He is in surgery. The doctors are doing the best they can."

Another cigarette. "My God." The words of the father were almost audible. "He's only five years old."

Standing on the edge of the canyon draws all of life into perspective. What matters and what doesn't are easily distinguished. Above the canyon wall no one is concerned about salaries or positions. No one asks about the car you drive or what part of town you live in. As aging humans stand beside this ageless chasm, all the games and disguises of life seem sadly silly.

It happened in one fiery instant.

"Where is the bird?" shouted a space engineer at Cape Canaveral.

"Oh, my God!" cried a teacher from the viewing stands nearby. "Don't let happen what I think just happened."

Confusion and horror raced through the nation as we stood on the edge of the canyon watching seven of our best disintegrate before our eyes as the shuttle exploded into a white and orange fireball.

Once again we were reminded that even at our technological finest, we are still frighteningly frail.

It is possible that I'm addressing someone who is walking the canyon wall. Someone you love dearly has been called into the unknown and you are alone. Alone with your fears and alone with your doubts. If this is the case, please read the rest of this piece very carefully. Look carefully at the scene described in John 11.

In this scene there are two people: Martha and Jesus. And for all practical purposes they are the only two people in the universe.

Her words were full of despair. "If you had been here…" She stares into the Master's face with confused eyes. She'd been strong long enough; now it hurt too badly. Lazarus was dead. Her brother was gone. And the one man who could have made a difference didn't. He hadn't even made it for the burial. Something about death makes us accuse God of betrayal. "If God were here there would be no death!" we claim.

You see, if God is God anywhere, he has to be God in the face of death. Pop psychology can deal with depression. Pep talks can deal with pessimism. Prosperity can handle hunger. But only God can deal with our ultimate dilemma—death. And only the God of the Bible has dared to stand on the canyon's edge and offer an answer. He has to be God in the face of death. If not, he is not God anywhere.

Jesus wasn't angry at Martha. Perhaps it was his patience that caused her to change her tone from frustration to earnestness. "Even now God will give you whatever you ask."

Jesus then made one of those claims that place him either on the throne or in the asylum: "Your brother will rise again."

Martha misunderstood. (Who wouldn't have?) "I know he will rise again in the resurrection at the last day."

That wasn't what Jesus meant. Don't miss the context of the next words. Imagine the setting: Jesus has intruded on the enemy's turf; he's standing in Satan's territory, Death Canyon. His stomach turns as he smells the sulfuric stench of the ex-angel, and he winces as he hears the oppressed wails of those trapped in the prison. Satan has been here. He has violated one of God's creations.

With his foot planted on the serpent's head, Jesus speaks loudly enough that his words echo off the canyon walls.

"I am the resurrection and the life. He who believes in me will live, even though he dies; and whoever lives and believes in me will never die" (John 11:25).

It is a hinge point in history. A chink has been found in death's armor. The keys to the halls of hell have been claimed. The buzzards scatter and the scorpions scurry as Life confronts death—and wins! The wind stops. A cloud blocks the sun and a bird chirps in the distance while a humiliated snake slithers between the rocks and disappears into the ground.

The stage has been set for a confrontation at Calvary.

But Jesus isn't through with Martha. With eyes locked on hers he asks the greatest question found in Scripture, a question meant as much for you and me as for Martha.

"Do you believe this?"

Wham! There it is. The bottom line. The dimension that separates Jesus from a thousand gurus and prophets who have come down the pike. The question that drives any responsible listener to absolute obedience to or total rejection of the Christian faith.

"Do you believe this?"

Let the question sink into your heart for a minute. Do you believe that a young, penniless itinerant is larger than your death? Do you truly believe that death is nothing more than an entrance ramp to a new highway?

"Do you believe this?"

Jesus didn't pose this query as a topic for discussion in Sunday schools. It was never intended to be dealt with while basking in the stained glass sunlight or while seated on padded pews.

No. This is a canyon question. A question which makes sense only during an all-night vigil or in the stillness of smoke-filled waiting rooms. A question that makes sense when all of our props, crutches, and costumes are taken away. For then we must face ourselves as we really are: rudderless humans tailspinning toward disaster. And we are forced to see him for what he claims to be: our only hope.

As much out of desperation as inspiration, Martha said yes. As she studied the tan face of that Galilean carpenter, something told her she'd probably never get closer to the truth than she was right now. So she gave him her hand and let him lead her away from the canyon wall.

"I am the resurrection and the life.... Do you believe this?"

CHAPTER 13

A TALE OF
TWO TREES

I

Formless masses. Floating. Disconnected.
Divine artist. Earthly dream.
Light! Sun rays piercing through jungle trees. Sunsets volcanic with explosions of gold. Soft sheets of moonlight soothing a weary ocean.

Beings! Snorting. Flying. Splashing. Bleating. Gnawing. Clawing. Digging.

Sound! Horse's hoof beats. Cawing crows. Hyena laughter. Cannoning thunder. Chirping chicks. Rat-tat-tatting rain.

Nothingness converted.

Then silence…as an unseen Sculptor molds mud and dust. Lions motionlessly watching. Sparrows perched, peering downward. Clouds hovering. Inquisitive kangaroos. Curious caribou. Snooping centipedes.

"What's he making?"

"An animal?"

Giraffes peeking through leaves. Squirrels chattering gossip. Pausing. Wondering. Gibbering.

"A mountain?"

A sudden breeze, surprisingly warm, whistles through the leaves scattering dust from the lifeless form. And with the breath of fresh air comes the difference. Winging on the warm wind is his image. Laughter is laid in the sculpted cheeks. A reservoir of tears is stored in the soul. A sprinkling of twinkle for the eyes. Poetry for the spirit. Logic. Loyalty. Like leaves on an autumn breeze, they float and land and are absorbed. His gifts become a part of him.

His Majesty smiles at his image. "It is good."

The eyes open.

Oneness. Creator and created walking on the river bank. Laughter. Purity. Innocent joy. Life unending.

Then the tree.

The struggle. The snake. The lie. The enticement. Heart torn, lured. Soul drawn to pleasure, to independence, to importance. Inner agony. Whose will?

The choice. Death of innocence. Entrance of death. The fall.

Tear stains mingling with fruit-stains.

II

The Quest.

"Abram, you will father a nation! And Abram—tell the people I love them."

"Moses, you will deliver my people! And Moses—tell the people I love them."

"Joshua, you will lead the chosen ones! And Joshua—tell the people I love them."

"David, you will reign over the people! And David—tell the people I love them."

"Jeremiah, you will bear tidings of bondage! But Jeremiah, remind my children, remind my children that I love them."

Altars. Sacrifices. Rebelling. Returning. Reacting. Repenting. Romance. Tablets. Judges. Pillars. Bloodshed. Wars. Kings. Giants. Law. Hezekiah. Nehemiah. Hosea... God watching, never turning, ever loving, ever yearning for the Garden again.

III

Empty throne. Spirit descending. Hushed angels.

A girl…
    a womb…
        an egg.

The same Divine Artist again forms a body. This time his own. Fleshly divinity. Skin layered on spirit. Omnipotence with hair. Toenails. Knuckles. Molars. Kneecaps. Once again he walks with man. Yet the Garden is now thorny. Thorns that cut, thorns that poison, thorns that remain lodged, leaving bitter wounds. Disharmony. Sickness. Betrayal. Fear. Guilt.

The lions no longer pause. The clouds no longer hover. The birds scatter too quickly. Disharmony. Competition. Blindness.

And once again, a tree.

Once again the struggle. The snake. The enticement. Heart torn, lured. Once again the question, "Whose will?"

Then the choice. Tear stains mingle with bloodstains. Relationship restored. Bridge erected.

Once again he smiles. "It is good."

For just as death came by means of a man, in the same way the rising from death comes by means of a man. For just as all men die because of their union to Adam, in the same way all will be raised to life because of their union to Christ.[1]

CHAPTER 14

NO ACCIDENT

I t has all the ingredients of a good sermon illustration. It's emotional. It's dramatic. And it's a story that'll break your heart. Heaven only knows how many times preachers have used it.

There's only one problem. It's not accurate.

Maybe you've heard it.

It's the story of an engineer who operated a drawbridge across a mighty river. With a control panel of levers and switches, he set into motion a monstrous set of gears that either lifted the bridge for the river traffic or closed it for the oncoming train.

One day he took his young son to work with him. The fascinated boy hurled question after question at his dad. It was not until the span had opened to allow the passage of a ship that the father noticed the questions had ceased and his son had left the room. He looked out the window of his control cabin and saw the young boy climbing on the teeth of the gears. As he hurried toward the machinery to get his son, he heard the whistle of an approaching train.

His pulse quickened. If he closed the bridge there would be no time to retrieve his son. He had to make a choice. Either his son would be killed or a trainload of innocent passengers would be killed. A horrible dilemma mandated a horrible decision. The engineer knew what he had to do. He reached for the lever.

A powerful story, isn't it? It's often used to describe the sacrifice of Christ. And it is not without its parallels. It's true that God could not save man without killing his son. The heart of God the Father did twist in grief as he slammed the gears of death down on Jesus. And it's sad, yet true, that the innocent have whizzed by the scene of the crime oblivious to the sacrifice that has just saved them from certain death.

But there is one inference in the story that's woefully in need of correction.

Read this quote from the first sermon ever preached about the cross and see if you can find the revealing phrase.

> Men of Israel, listen to this: Jesus of Nazareth was a man accredited by God to you by miracles, wonders and signs, which God did among you through him, as you yourselves know. This man was handed over to you by God's set purpose and foreknowledge; and you, with the help of wicked men, put him to death by nailing him to the cross.[1]

Did you see it? It's the solemn phrase in the paragraph. It's the statement that rings of courage, the one with roots that extend back to eternity. It is the phrase which, perhaps as much as any in the Bible, describes the real price God paid to adopt you.

Which phrase? "God's set purpose and foreknowledge." The Revised Standard Version calls it "the definite plan and foreknowledge of God." Today's English Version translates the phrase, "In accordance with his own plan." Regardless how you phrase it, the truth is ever so sobering: The cross was no accident.

Jesus' death was not the result of a panicking, cosmological engineer. The cross wasn't a tragic surprise. Calvary was not a knee-jerk response to a world plummeting towards destruction. It wasn't a patch-job or a stop-gap measure. The death of the Son of God was anything but an unexpected peril.

No, it was part of a plan. It was a calculated choice. "It was the LORD's will to crush him."[2] The cross was drawn into the original blueprint. It was written into the script. The moment the forbidden fruit touched the lips of Eve, the shadow of a cross appeared on the horizon. And between that moment and the moment the man with the mallet placed the spike against the wrist of God, a master plan was fulfilled.

What does that mean? It means Jesus planned his own sacrifice.

It means Jesus intentionally planted the tree from which his cross would be carved.

It means he willingly placed the iron ore in the heart of the earth from which the nails would be cast.

It means he voluntarily placed his Judas in the womb of a woman.

It means Christ was the one who set in motion the political machinery that would send Pilate to Jerusalem.

And it also means he didn't have to do it—but he did.

It was no accident—would that it had been! Even the cruelest of criminals is spared the agony of having his death sentence read to him before his life even begins.

But Jesus was born crucified. Whenever he became conscious of who he was, he also became conscious of what he had to do. The cross-shaped shadow could always be seen. And the screams of hell's imprisoned could always be heard.

This explains the glint of determination on his face as he turned to go to Jerusalem for the last time. He was on his death march.[3]

This explains the resoluteness in the words, "The reason my Father loves me is that I lay down my life—only to take it up again. No one takes it from me, but I lay it down of my own accord."[4]

It explains the enigmatic question, "Does this offend you? What if you see the Son of Man ascend to where he was before!"[5]

The cross explains…

Why he told the Pharisees that the "goal" of his life would be fulfilled only on the third day after his death.[6]

The mysterious appearance of Moses and Elijah on the Mount of Transfiguration to discuss his "departure."[7] They'd come to offer one last word of encouragement.

Why John the Baptist introduced Jesus to the crowds as the "Lamb of God, who takes away the sin of the world!"[8]

Maybe it's why he tore the grass out by the roots in Gethsemane. He knew the hell he'd endure for saying, "Thy will be done."

Maybe the cross was why he so loved children. They represented the very thing he would have to give: Life.

It adds gravity to his prophecies, "I lay down my life for the sheep."[9] "Jesus began to explain to his disciples that he must go to Jerusalem and suffer many things at the hands of elders, chief priests and teachers of the law, and that he must be killed and on the third day be raised to life."[10]

The reference to the rejected stone,[11] the anointing for burial,[12] the dismissal of Judas from the Last Supper:[13] All of these incidents take on a sobering dimension when the imminence of the cross is considered. Our Master lived a three-dimensional life. He had as clear a view of the future as he did of the present and the past.

This is why the ropes used to tie his hands and the soldiers used to lead him to the cross were unnecessary. They were incidental. Had they not been there, had there been no trial, no Pilate and no crowd, the very same crucifixion would have occurred. Had Jesus been forced to nail himself to the cross, he would have done it. For it was not the soldiers who killed him, nor the screams of the mob: It was his devotion to us.

So call it what you wish: An act of grace. A plan of redemption. A martyr's sacrifice. But whatever you call it, don't call it an accident. It was anything but that.

Chapter 15

Rediscovering Amazement

"I am with you always…"
MATTHEW 28:20

From where I write I can see several miracles. White-crested waves slap the beach with rhythmic regularity. One after the other the rising swells of salt water gain momentum, humping, rising, then standing to salute the beach before crashing onto the sand. How many billions of times has this simple mystery repeated itself since time began?

In the distance lies a miracle of colors—twins of blue. The ocean-blue of the Atlantic encounters the pale blue of the sky, separated only by the horizon, stretched like a taut wire between two poles.

Also within my eyesight are the two bookends of life. A young mother pushes a baby in a carriage, both recent participants with God in the miracle of birth. They pass a snowy-haired, stooped old gentleman seated on a bench, a victim of life's thief—age. (I wonder if he is aware of the curtain closing on his life.)

Behind them are three boys kicking a soccer ball on the beach. With effortless skill they coordinate countless muscles and reflexes, engage and disengage perfectly designed joints…all to do one task—move a ball in the sand.

Miracles. Divine miracles.

These are miracles because they are mysteries. Scientifically explainable? Yes. Reproducible? To a degree.

But still they are mysteries. Events that stretch beyond our understanding and find their origins in another realm. They are every bit as divine as divided seas, walking cripples, and empty tombs.

And they are as much a reminder of God's presence as were the walking lame, fleeing demons, and silenced storms. They are miracles. They are signs. They are testimonies. They are instantaneous incarnations. They remind us of the same truth: The unseen is now visible. The distant has drawn near. His Majesty has come to be seen. And he is in the most common of earth's corners.

In fact, it is the normality not the uniqueness of God's miracles that causes them to be so staggering. Rather than shocking the globe with an occasional demonstration of deity, God has opted to display his power daily. Proverbially. Pounding waves. Prism-cast colors. Birth, death, life. We are surrounded by miracles. God is throwing testimonies at us like fireworks, each one exploding, "God is! God is!"

The psalmist marveled at such holy handiwork. "Where can I go from your Spirit?" he questioned with delight. "Where can I flee from your presence? If I go up to the heavens, you are there; if I make my bed in the depths, you are there."[1]

We wonder, with so many miraculous testimonies around us, how we could escape God. But somehow we do. We live in an art gallery of divine creativity and yet are content to gaze only at the carpet.

Or what is pathetically worse, we demand *more*. More signs. More proof. More hat tricks. As if God were some vaudeville magician we could summon for a dollar.

How have we grown so deaf? How have we grown so immune to awesomeness? Why are we so reluctant to be staggered or thunderstruck?

Perhaps the frequency of the miracles blinds us to their beauty. After all, what spice is there in a springtime or a tree blossom? Don't the seasons come every year? Aren't there countless seashells just like this one?

Bored, we say Ho-hum and replace the remarkable with the regular, the unbelievable with the anticipated. Science and statistics wave their unmagic wand across the face of life, squelching the oohs and aahs and replacing them with formulas and figures.

Would you like to see Jesus? Do you dare be an eyewitness of His Majesty? Then rediscover amazement.

The next time you hear a baby laugh or see an ocean wave, take note. Pause and listen as His Majesty whispers ever so gently, "I'm here."

CHAPTER 16

HOPE

It's one of the most compelling narratives in all of Scripture. So fascinating is the scene, in fact, that Luke opted to record it in detail. Two disciples are walking down the dusty road to the village of Emmaus. Their talk concerns the crucified Jesus. Their words come slowly, trudging in cadence with the dirge-like pace of their feet.

"I can hardly believe it. He's gone."

"What do we do now?"

"It's Peter's fault, he shouldn't have…"

Just then a stranger comes up from behind and says, "I'm sorry, but I couldn't help overhearing you. Who are you discussing?"

They stop and turn. Other travelers make their way around them as the three stand in silence. Finally one of them asks, "Where have you been the last few days? Haven't you heard about Jesus of Nazareth?" And he continues to tell what has happened.[1]

This scene fascinates me—two sincere disciples telling how the last nail has been driven in Israel's coffin. God, in disguise, listens patiently, his wounded hands buried deeply in his robe. He must have been touched at the faithfulness of this pair. Yet he also must have been a bit chagrined. He had just gone to hell and back to give heaven to earth, and these two were worried about the political situation of Israel.

"But we had hoped that he was the one who was going to redeem Israel."

But we had hoped… How often have you heard a phrase like that?

"We were hoping the doctor would release him."

"I had hoped to pass the exam."

"We had hoped the surgery would get all the tumor."

"I thought the job was in the bag."

Words painted gray with disappointment. What we wanted didn't come. What came, we didn't want. The result? Shattered hope. The foundation of our world trembles.

We trudge up the road to Emmaus dragging our sandals in the dust, wondering what we did to deserve such a plight. "What kind of God would let me down like this?"

And yet, so tear-filled are our eyes and so limited is our perspective that God could be the fellow walking next to us and we wouldn't know it.

You see, the problem with our two heavy-hearted friends was not a lack of faith, but a lack of vision. Their petitions were limited to what they could imagine—an earthly kingdom. Had God answered their prayer, had he granted their hope, the Seven-Day War would have started two thousand years earlier and Jesus would have spent the next forty years training his apostles to be cabinet members. You have to wonder if God's most merciful act is his refusal to answer some of our prayers.

We are not much different than burdened travelers, are we? We roll in the mud of self-pity in the very shadow of the cross. We piously ask for his will and then have the audacity to pout if everything doesn't go our way. If we would just remember the heavenly body that awaits us, we'd stop complaining that he hasn't healed this earthly one.

Our problem is not so much that God doesn't give us what we hope for as it is that we don't know the right thing for which to hope. (You may want to read that sentence again.)

Hope is not what you expect; it is what you would never dream. It is a wild, improbable tale with a pinch-me-I'm-dreaming ending. It's Abraham adjusting his bifocals so he can see not his grandson, but his son. It's Moses standing in the promised land not with Aaron or Miriam at his side, but with Elijah and the transfigured Christ. It's Zechariah left speechless at the sight of his wife Elizabeth, gray-headed and pregnant. And it is the two Emmaus-bound pilgrims reaching out to take a piece of bread only to see that the hands from which it is offered are pierced.

Hope is not a granted wish or a favor performed; no, it is far greater than that. It is a zany, unpredictable dependence on a God who loves to surprise us out of our socks and be there in the flesh to see our reaction.

CHAPTER 17

ETERNAL
INSTANTS

We played every game we knew. We ran up and down the hall. We played "find me" behind the couch. We bounced the beach ball off each other's heads. We wrestled, played tag, and danced. It was a big evening for Mom, Dad, and little Jenna. We were having so much fun that we ignored the bedtime hour and turned off the TV. And if the storm hadn't hit, who knows how late we would have played.

But the storm hit. Rain pattered, then tapped, then slapped against the windows. The winds roared in off the Atlantic and gushed through the nearby mountains with such force that all the power went off. The adjacent valley acted as a funnel, hosing wind and rain on the city.

We all went into the bedroom and laid on the bed. In the darkness we listened to the divine orchestra. Electricity danced in the sky like a conductor's baton summoning the deep kettle drums of thunder.

I sensed it as we were lying on the bed. It blew over me mixed with the sweet fragrance of fresh rain. My wife was lying silently at my side. Jenna was using my stomach for her pillow. She, too, was quiet. Our second child, only a month from birth, rested within the womb of her mother. They must have sensed it, for no one spoke. It entered our presence as if introduced by God himself. And no one dared stir for fear it leave prematurely.

What was it? An eternal instant.

An instant in time that had no time. A picture that froze in midframe, demanding to be savored. A minute that refused to die after sixty seconds. A moment that was lifted off the timeline and amplified into a forever so all the angels could witness its majesty.

An eternal instant.

A moment that reminds you of the treasures surrounding you. Your home. Your peace of mind. Your health. A moment that tenderly rebukes you for spending so much time on temporal preoccupations such as savings accounts, houses, and punctuality. A moment that can bring a mist to the manliest of eyes and perspective to the darkest life.

Eternal instants have dotted history.

It was an eternal instant when the Creator smiled and said, "It is good." It was a timeless moment when Abraham pleaded for mercy from the God of mercy, "But if there are just ten faithful." It was a moment without time when Noah pushed open the rain-soaked hatch and breathed in the clean air. And it was a moment in the "fullness of time" when a carpenter, some smelly shepherds, and an exhausted young mother stood in silent awe at the sight of the infant in the manger.

Eternal instants. You've had them. We all have.

Sharing a porch swing on a summer evening with your grandchild.

Seeing her face in the glow of a candle.

Putting your arm into your husband's as you stroll through the golden leaves and breathe the brisk autumn air.

Listening to your six-year-old thank God for everything from goldfish to Grandma.

Such moments are necessary because they remind us that everything is okay. The King is still on the throne and life is still worth living. Eternal instants remind us that love is still the greatest possession and the future is nothing to fear.

The next time an instant in your life begins to be eternal, let it. Put your head back on the pillow and soak it in. Resist the urge to cut it short. Don't interrupt the silence or shatter the solemnity. You are, in a very special way, on holy ground.

CHAPTER 18

WHAT DO
YOU SEE?

"Anyone who has seen me has seen the Father."
JOHN 14:9

S hould a man see only popularity, he becomes a mirror, reflecting whatever needs to be reflected to gain acceptance. Though in vogue, he is vague. Though in style, he is stodgy. Personal convictions change with the seasons. Individual beliefs come in all colors, each for a different night of the week. He's a puppet on a thousand strings. He's a singer of a hundred songs, with no song of his own. His appearance changes to fit the setting so often that he forgets who he set out to be. He is everyone and no one.

Should a man see only power, he becomes a wolf—prowling, hunting, and stalking the elusive game. Recognition is his prey and people are his prizes. His quest is endless. There is always another world to conquer or another person to control. As a result, he who sees only power is degraded to an animal, an insatiable scavenger controlled not by a will from within but by lurings from without.

Should a man see only pleasure, he becomes a carnival thrill-seeker, alive only in bright lights, wild rides, and titillating entertainment. With lustful fever he races from ride to ride, satisfying his insatiable passion for sensations only long enough to look for another. Ferris wheels of romance. Haunted houses of eroticism. Hammer rides of danger and excitement. Long after the crowd is gone he can still be found on the carnival grounds rummaging through empty boxes of popcorn and sticky cones that held the cotton candy. He is driven by passion, willing to sell his soul if need be for one more rush, one more race of the pulse, one more sideshow that will take him away from the real world of promises broken and commitments to keep.

Seekers of popularity, power, and pleasure. The end result is the same: painful unfulfillment.

Only in seeing his Maker does a man truly become man. For in seeing his Creator man catches a glimpse of what he was intended to be. He who would see his God would then see the reason for death and the purpose of time. Destiny? Tomorrow? Truth? All are questions within the reach of the man who knows his source.

It is in seeing Jesus that man sees his Source.

PART TWO

OUR IMITATION

A student…
who is fully trained
will be like his teacher.

LUKE 6:40

CHAPTER 19

HE FORGOT

I was thanking the Father today for his mercy. I began listing the sins he'd forgiven. One by one I thanked God for forgiving my stumbles and tumbles. My motives were pure and my heart was thankful, but my understanding of God was wrong. It was when I used the word *remember* that it hit me.

"Remember the time I..." I was about to thank God for another act of mercy. But I stopped. Something was wrong. The word *remember* seemed displaced. It was an off-key note in a sonata, a misspelled word in a poem. It was a baseball game in December. It didn't fit. "Does he remember?"

Then *I* remembered. I remembered his words. "And I will remember their sins no more."[1]

Wow! Now, *that* is a remarkable promise.

God doesn't just forgive, he forgets. He erases the board. He destroys the evidence. He burns the microfilm. He clears the computer.

He doesn't remember my mistakes. For all the things he does do, this is one thing he refuses to do. He refuses to keep a list of my wrongs. When I ask for forgiveness he doesn't pull out a clipboard and say, "But I've already forgiven him for that five hundred and sixteen times."

He doesn't remember.

"As far as the east is from the west, so far has he removed our transgressions from us."[2]

"I will be merciful toward their iniquities."[3]

"Even if you are stained as red as crimson, I can make you white as wool!"[4]

No, he doesn't remember. But I do, you do. You still remember. You're like me. You still remember what you did before you changed. In the cellar of your heart lurk the ghosts of yesterday's sins. Sins you've confessed; errors of which you've repented; damage you've done your best to repair.

And though you're a different person, the ghosts still linger. Though you've locked the basement door, they still haunt you. They float to meet you, spooking your soul and robbing your joy. With wordless whispers they remind you of moments when you forgot whose child you were.

That horrid lie.

That business trip you took away from home, that took you so far away from home.

The time you exploded in anger.

Those years spent in the hollow of Satan's hand.

That day you were needed, but didn't respond.

That date.

That jealousy.

That habit.

Poltergeists from yesterday's pitfalls. Spiteful specters that slyly suggest, "Are you really forgiven? Sure, God forgets most of our mistakes, but do you think he could actually forget the time you…"

As a result, your spiritual walk has a slight limp. Oh, you're still faithful. You still do all the right things and say all the right words. But just when you begin to make strides, just when your wings begin to spread and you prepare to soar like an eagle, the ghost appears. It emerges from the swamps of your soul and causes you to question yourself.

"You can't teach a Bible class with your background."

"You, a missionary?"

"How dare you ask him to come to church. What if he finds out about the time you fell away?"

"Who are *you* to offer help?"

The ghost spews waspish words of accusation, deafening your ears to the promises of the cross. And it flaunts your failures in your face, blocking your vision of the Son and leaving you the shadow of a doubt.

Now, honestly. Do you think God sent that ghost? Do you think

God is the voice that reminds you of the putridness of your past? Do you think God was teasing when he said, "I will remember your sins no more?" Was he exaggerating when he said he would cast our sins as far as the east is from the west? Do you actually believe he would make a statement like "I will not hold their iniquities against them" and then rub our noses in them whenever we ask for help?

Of course you don't. You and I just need an occasional reminder of God's nature, his forgetful nature.

To love conditionally is against God's nature. Just as it's against your nature to eat trees and against mine to grow wings, it's against God's nature to remember forgiven sins.

You see, God is either the God of perfect grace…or he is not God. Grace forgets. Period. He who is perfect love cannot hold grudges. If he does, then he isn't perfect love. And if he isn't perfect love, you might as well put this book down and go fishing, because both of us are chasing fairy tales.

But I believe in his loving forgetfulness. And I believe he has a graciously terrible memory.

Think about this. If he didn't forget, how could we pray? How could we sing to him? How could we dare enter into his presence if the moment he saw us he remembered all our pitiful past? How could we enter his throne room wearing the rags of our selfishness and gluttony? We couldn't.

And we don't. Read this powerful passage from Paul's letter to the Galatians and watch your pulse rate. You're in for a thrill. "For as many of you as were baptized into Christ have *put on* Christ."[5]

You read it right. We have "put on" Christ. When God looks at us he doesn't see us; he sees Christ. We "wear" him. We are hidden in him; we are covered by him. As the song says, "Dressed in his righteousness alone, faultless to stand before the throne."

Presumptuous, you say? Sacrilegious? It would be if it were my idea. But it isn't; it's his. We are presumptuous not when we marvel at his grace, but when we reject it. And we're sacrilegious not when we claim his forgiveness, but when we allow the haunting sins of yesterday to convince us that God forgives but he doesn't forget.

Do yourself a favor. Purge your cellar. Exorcise your basement. Take the Roman nails of Calvary and board up the door.

And remember...he forgot.

CHAPTER 20

FACING THE FACTS

I am writing in a hospital room.

I am sitting in one of those uncomfortable vinyl chairs that convert into an uncomfortable vinyl guest bed. Just a few feet from me sleeps my wife. She's minus one gallbladder. We've been here for four days (almost 100 hours). Denalyn is recovering well. But because of the medication she's sleepy most of the time, so I've had a good opportunity to do some observing. And I've come to a conclusion. And since she is asleep and the nurse doesn't seem too conversant, I think I'll write down my conclusion. Want to read it?

A hospital is a microcosm of the world.

Why? Let me explain.

On the surface, a hospital appears to be a great place. The sheets are clean and the staff is friendly. Nurses come and go with warm smiles. Doctors periodically appear wearing nice loafers, a tie, and a kind face. Friends and family visit bringing pretty plants and friendly words.

There's a curiously large number of smiles here. I've walked the halls and been greeted by the smiling Candy Stripers pushing the coffee cart. The gift shop downstairs is full of magazines with smiling people on the covers. The lady selling them smiled broadly at me when I bought one. The receptionist at the front desk smiles when you pass by.

Along with the smiles and the comfort is the escape hatch. The TV is placed near the ceiling and through it you can climb into the outside world. Just flip the switch and you are riding on the Love Boat or watching the Yankees game.

Smiles, efficiency, distraction. I've seen some resorts that don't offer this kind of treatment. My, you almost forget where you are.

In fact, were it not for the undisguiseable reminders, you would forget. But just when you relax—just when you begin to smile to yourself, just when you giggle at Bill Cosby—a siren reminds you. The scream of the patient next door reminds you. Paramedics rushing a stretcher toward the emergency room remind you.

And the reminder is sobering. This is a hospital. The sole function of this building is to bargain with death. The walls can't be white enough nor the staff polite enough to hide the stark reality of the bottom line: People come here to give all they have to postpone the inevitable.

We give it our best shot. We put up the best we have—the best technology, the best minds, the best equipment; and yet, at best we walk away with an extension, never a solution. And though we may walk or be wheeled out with smiles and waves of victory, down deep we know it is just a matter of time until the best we have won't be enough and the enemy will conquer.

So a hospital is a paradoxical place. A place where the reality is hidden, yet can't be hidden because the reality is too real.

You saw the same today in your world, didn't you? The script was the same; only the props were different. That's why I reached my conclusion—our world is identical to a hospital. Have you ever noticed the endless extremes to which a person will go to hide the realities of life?

Take age for example. Do you know anyone who has not aged? Do you know anyone who is younger today than when you met him? Aging is a universal condition. But the way we try to hide it, you would think it was a plague!

There are girdles which compact the middle-age spread for both sexes. There are hair transplants, wigs, toupees, and hair pieces. Dentures bring youth to the mouth, wrinkle cream brings youth to the face, and color in a bottle brings youth to the hair.

All to hide what everyone already knows—we're getting older.

Death is another lump in the carpet. We don't like it. (If you ever want to stall a conversation at a party just say, "How are you feeling about your approaching death?" It won't put much life into the conversation.)

I have a friend who has cancer. At present the cancer is in remission. Recently he had to go to the doctor for a physical. A nurse, apparently unaware of his condition, was asking him questions for his medical record. "Are you presently ill?"

"Well, yes. I have cancer."

She dropped her pencil and looked up at him. "Are you terminal?" she asked.

"Yes, aren't we all?"

You'd think we weren't, the way the subject is kept hush-hush.

We also try to disguise ourselves. It's wild. People from the country try to look like they're from the city and people from the city try to look like they're from the country. We change our accents, change our noses; we even try to change our names—all to avoid facing who we are.

But this obsession with fleeing the facts is as maddening as it is futile. For, as in the case of the hospital, the truth always surfaces. A siren sounds causing reality to shock us out of our sleep.

An old college roomie retires and you have to admit that if he is in the autumn of his life, you must be too.

You walk your daughter down the aisle. "When did she grow up?"

You wake up in an emergency room to the beeping of a machine and find wires suction-cupped to your chest.

Be the event pleasant or painful, the result is the same. Reality breaks through the papier-mâché mask and screams at you like a Marine drill sergeant. "You *are* getting old! You *are* going to die! You can't be someone you are not!"

The props are kicked away and you tumble head over feet, crashing onto the hard floor of the facts of life. You might as well turn off the TV and take off the new outfit. Reality has reared its head like the Loch Ness monster and you can no longer deny its existence.

The best thing for you to do now is pause and think. Take a good look at the facts. And while you're looking at them, it would be wise to take a good look at him. To those perched on the peak of Mount Perspective, His Majesty takes on special significance.

Jesus does his best work at such moments. Just when the truth about life sinks in, his truth starts to surface. He takes us by the hand and dares us not to sweep the facts under the rug but to confront them with him at our side.

Aging? A necessary process to pass on to a better world.

Death? Merely a brief passage, a tunnel.

Self? Designed and created for a purpose, purchased by God himself. There, was that so bad?

Funerals, divorces, illnesses, and stays in the hospital—you can't lie about life at such times. Maybe that's why he's always present at such moments.

The next time you find yourself alone in a dark alley facing the undeniables of life, don't cover them with a blanket, or ignore them with a nervous grin. Don't turn up the TV and pretend they aren't there. Instead, stand still, whisper his name, and listen. He is nearer than you think.

CHAPTER 21

LIGHT OF THE... STORAGE CLOSET?

few nights ago a peculiar thing happened.

An electrical storm caused a blackout in our neighborhood. When the lights went out, I felt my way through the darkness into the storage closet where we keep the candles for nights like this. Through the glow of a lit match I looked up on the shelf where the candles were stored. There they were, already positioned in their stands, melted to various degrees by previous missions. I took my match and lit four of them.

How they illuminated the storage room! What had been a veil of blackness suddenly radiated with soft, golden light! I could see the freezer I had just bumped with my knee. And I could see my tools that needed to be straightened.

"How great it is to have light!" I said out loud, and then spoke to the candles. "If you do such a good job here in the storage closet, just wait till I get you out where you're really needed! I'll put one of you on the table so we can eat. I'll put one of you on my desk so I can read. I'll give one of you to Denalyn so she can cross-stitch. And I'll set you," I took down the largest one, "in the living room where you can light up the whole area." (I felt a bit foolish talking to candles—but what do you do when the lights go out?)

I was turning to leave with the large candle in my hand when I heard a voice, "Now, hold it right there."

I stopped. *Somebody's in here!* I thought. Then I relaxed. *It's just Denalyn, teasing me for talking to the candles.*

"OK, honey, cut the kidding," I said in the semidarkness. No answer.

Hmm, maybe it was the wind. I took another step.

"Hold it, I said!" There was that voice. My hands began to sweat.

"Who said that?"

"I did." The voice was near my hand.

"Who are you? What are you?"

"I'm a candle." I looked at the candle I was holding. It was burning a strong, golden flame. It was red and sat on a heavy wooden candle holder that had a firm handle.

I looked around once more to see if the voice could be coming from another source. "There's no one here but you, me, and the rest of us candles," the voice informed me.

I lifted up the candle to take a closer look. You won't believe what I saw. There was a tiny face in the wax. (I told you you wouldn't believe me.) Not just a wax face that someone had carved, but a moving, functioning, fleshlike face full of expression and life.

"Don't take me out of here!"

"What?"

"I said, don't take me out of this room."

"What do you mean? I have to take you out. You're a candle. Your job is to give light. It's dark out there. People are stubbing their toes and walking into walls. You have to come out and light up the place!"

"But you can't take me out. I'm not ready," the candle explained with pleading eyes. "I need more preparation."

I couldn't believe my ears. "More preparation?"

"Yeah, I've decided I need to research this job of light-giving so I won't go out and make a bunch of mistakes. You'd be surprised how distorted the glow of an untrained candle can be. So I'm doing some studying. I just finished a book on wind resistance. I'm in the middle of a great series of tapes on wick build-up and conservation—and I'm reading the new bestseller on flame display. Have you heard of it?"

"No," I answered.

"You might like it. It's called *Waxing Eloquently.*"

"That really sounds inter—" I caught myself. *What am I doing? I'm in here conversing with a candle while my wife and daughters are out there in the darkness!*

"All right then," I said. "You're not the only candle on the shelf. I'll blow you out and take the others!"

But just as I got my cheeks full of air, I heard other voices.

"We aren't going either!"

It was a conspiracy. I turned around and looked at the three other candles; each with flames dancing above a miniature face.

I was beyond feeling awkward about talking to candles. I was getting miffed.

"You are candles and your job is to light dark places!"

"Well, that may be what you think," said the candle on the far left— a long, thin fellow with a goatee and a British accent. "*You* may think we have to go, but I'm busy."

"Busy?"

"Yes, I'm meditating."

"What? A candle that meditates?"

"Yes. I'm meditating on the importance of light. It's really enlightening."

I decided to reason with them. "Listen, I appreciate what you guys are doing. I'm all for meditation time. And everyone needs to study and research; but for goodness' sake, you guys have been in here for weeks! Haven't you had enough time to get your wick on straight?"

"And you other two," I asked, "are you going to stay in here as well?"

A short, fat, purple candle with plump cheeks that reminded me of Santa Claus spoke up. "I'm waiting to get my life together. I'm not stable enough. I lose my temper easily. I guess you could say that I'm a hot-head."

The last candle had a female voice, very pleasant to the ear. "I'd like to help," she explained, "but lighting the darkness is not my gift."

All this was sounding too familiar. "Not your gift? What do you mean?"

"Well, I'm a singer. I sing to other candles to encourage them to burn more brightly." Without asking my permission, she began a rendition of "This Little Light of Mine." (I have to admit, she had a good voice.)

The other three joined in, filling the storage room with singing.

"Hey," I shouted above the music, "I don't mind if you sing while you work! In fact, we could use a little music out there!"

They didn't hear me. They were singing too loudly. I yelled louder.

"Come on, you guys. There's plenty of time for this later. We've got a crisis on our hands."

They wouldn't stop. I put the big candle on the shelf and took a step back and considered the absurdity of it all. Four perfectly healthy candles singing to each other about light but refusing to come out of the closet. I had all I could take. One by one I blew them out. They kept singing to the end. The last one to flicker was the female. I snuffed her out right in the "puff" part of "Won't let Satan puff me out."

I stuck my hands in my pocket and walked back out in the darkness. I bumped my knee on the same freezer. Then I bumped into my wife.

"Where are the candles?" she asked.

"They don't...they won't work. Where did you buy those candles anyway?"

"Oh, they're church candles. Remember the church that closed down across town? I bought them there."

I understood.

CHAPTER 22

BLIND AMBITION

The scene is almost spooky: a tall, unfinished tower looming solitarily on a dusty plain. Its base is wide and strong but covered with weeds. Large stones originally intended for use in the tower lie forsaken on the ground. Buckets, hammers, and pulleys—all lie abandoned. The silhouette cast by the structure is lean and lonely.

Not too long ago, this tower was buzzing with activity. A bystander would have been impressed with the smooth-running construction of the world's first skyscraper. One group of workers stirred freshly made mortar. Another team pulled bricks out of the oven. A third group carried the bricks to the construction site while a fourth shouldered the load up a winding path to the top of the tower where it was firmly set in place.

It was a human anthill. Each worker knew his job and did it well.

Their dream was a tower. A tower that would be taller than anyone had ever dreamed. A tower that would punch through the clouds and scratch the heavens. And what was the purpose of the tower? To glorify God? No. To try to find God? No. To call people to look upward to God? Try again. To provide a heavenly haven of prayer? Still wrong.

The purpose of the work caused its eventual abortion. The method was right. The plan was effective. But the motive was wrong. Dead wrong. Read these minutes from the "Tower Planning Committee Meeting" and see what I mean:

"Come, let us build ourselves a city, and a tower with its top in the heavens, and [watch out] *let us make a name for ourselves.*"[1]

Why was the tower being built? Selfishness. Pure, 100 percent selfishness. The bricks were made of inflated egos and the mortar was made of pride. Men were giving sweat and blood for a pillar. Why? So that somebody's name could be remembered.

We have a name for that: blind ambition. Success at all cost. Becoming a legend in one's own time. Climbing the ladder to the top. King of the mountain. Top of the heap. "I did it my way."

We make heroes out of people who are ambitious. We hold them up as models for our kids and put their pictures on the covers of our magazines.

And rightly so. This world would be in sad shape without people who dream of touching the heavens. Ambition is that grit in the soul which creates disenchantment with the ordinary and puts the dare into dreams.

But left unchecked it becomes an insatiable addiction to power and prestige; a roaring hunger for achievement that devours people as a lion devours an animal, leaving behind only the skeletal remains of relationships.

The classic examples of nearsighted tower builders come to mind quickly. You'll recognize them, perhaps too well.

The husband who feeds his career with twelve-hour days, flight schedules, and apologies for being gone so much. "But it's just a matter of time, and I'll get my feet on the ground."

The social-conscious mother of three who never misses a chance to serve on a committee or attend a luncheon. "It's all for a good cause," she fools herself.

"I'll only need to do it this once," justifies the salesman as he lies about his product. Anything to get to the top of the tower.

Blind ambition. Distorted values.

The result? Rootless lives bouncing like tumbleweeds through ghost towns. Abandoned dreams. Crumbling homes. Windswept futures. All with one thing in common: a half-finished tower that stands as a stirring epitaph to those who follow.

God won't tolerate it. He didn't then and he won't now. He took the "Climb to Heaven Campaign" into his hands. With one sweep he painted the tower gray with confusion and sent workers babbling in all directions. He took man's greatest achievement and blew it into the winds like a child blows a dandelion.

Are you building any towers? Examine your motives. And remember the statement imprinted on the base of the windswept Tower of Babel: Blind ambition is a giant step away from God and one step closer to catastrophe.

CHAPTER 23

WARNINGS

I was mad. Real mad. The kind of mad that makes your jaw ache. But I had no one to be mad at except myself.

I'd seen that silly light burning on the car panel for days. And for days I'd ignored it. Too busy. "I'll take the car to the mechanic tomorrow." But tomorrow never became today. The light continued to burn, vainly waving red flags before my blind eyes. Something was wrong, but I had too many things to do.

"Next time I'll pay attention," I mumbled to myself. The flashlight I was waving must have looked like a dancing firefly to the oncoming traffic. The situation was not pretty: a cold winter night, stranded on a lonely highway in rural Brazil with my daughter and pregnant wife.

My breath became smoke as I stood on the shoulder flagging cars. I promised myself I would never ignore a warning again.

Warnings. Red lights in life that signal us of impending danger. They exist in all parts of life. Sirens scream as a marriage starts to sour; alarms blare when a faith weakens; flares go up to alert us of morals being compromised.

They manifest themselves in a variety of ways: guilt, depression, rationalizations. A friend might confront. A Scripture might sting. A burden might prove too heavy. Regardless of how they may arrive, warnings come with the same purpose: To alert. To wake up.

Unfortunately, they are not always heeded. All of us have learned to cover our ears and shield our eyes at the right moment. It's amazing how adept we can be at keeping them out. Warnings can be as blunt as a sledgehammer and we still turn our heads and whistle them away. We have just enough of the rascal in us to believe we are the proverbial exception to the rule.

It's as if there were a miniature receptionist in our brain instructed to intercept all warnings and file them in appropriate files. Can you imagine the scene?

"Hello. Screening department. May I help you?"

"Yes. This is the safety spectrum. I'm calling to advise Mr. Lucado that he is driving too fast."

"I'm sorry. Mr. Lucado left instructions that that particular warning was for the 'other guy' who isn't as experienced on highways."

Or,

"Hello, Headquarters? This is the health department. Please advise Mr. Lucado that he is in desperate need of rest."

"I certainly will…tomorrow."

Or perhaps,

"This is Mr. Lucado's conscience calling."

"I'm sorry, Mr. Lucado left word that he is having his horizon expanded and doesn't plan to return your call."

Or,

"This is the Conviction Section. I need to arrange for Mr. Lucado to read the Book of James within the next twenty-four hours. There are a couple of things he needs to remember."

"Let me check his schedule…hmmm. The next time Mr. Lucado is free to read the Bible is next month. However, he does have several golf games scheduled. Is there any way you can talk to him on the golf course?"

Even,

"This is Mr. Lucado's faith calling to remind him—hello? Hello? That's strange, I've been disconnected."

Warnings flash about us unheeded while we doze in the canoe floating down the Niagara River.

We're often surprised at life's mishaps, but when pressed against the wall of honesty we have to admit that if we had just fired that silly receptionist and done something about those calls, we could have avoided many problems. We usually knew that trouble was just around the bend. Christians who have fallen away felt the fire waning long before it went out. Unwanted pregnancies or explosions of anger may appear to be the fruit of a moment's waywardness, but in reality, they're usually the result of a history of ignoring warnings about an impending fire.

Are you close to the falls? Are your senses numb? Are your eyes trained to turn and roll when they should pause and observe?

Then maybe you need to repair your warning detector. Tune it up with a few cautions from Scripture. Be careful about—

Sticking your nose in other people's business:

> Like one who seizes a dog by the ears is a passer-by who meddles in a quarrel not his own.[1]

One-night stands:

> For a prostitute will bring a man to poverty, and an adulteress may cost him his very life. Can a man hold fire against his chest and not be burned? Can he walk on hot coals and not blister his feet? So it is with the man who commits adultery with another's wife. He shall not go unpunished for this sin.[2]

Dust-covered Bibles:

> We must pay more careful attention, therefore, to what we have heard, so that we do not drift away.[3]

Secret scampering that you think will go unnoticed:

> Do not be deceived: God cannot be mocked. A man reaps what he sows.[4]

Poor selection of a mate:

> It is better to dwell in the wilderness, than with a contentious and angry woman.[5]

The poisoning effect of gossip:

> The words of a gossip are like choice morsels; they go down
> to a man's inmost parts.[6]

Careless choice of companions:

> Bad company corrupts good character.[7]

Denial of Christ:

> Whoever disowns me before men, I will disown him before
> my Father in heaven.[8]

The lack of parental discipline:

> Do not withhold correction from a child, for if you beat him
> with a rod, he will not die. You shall beat him with a rod,
> and deliver his soul from hell.[9]

And three warnings about ignoring warnings:

> Cease listening to instruction, my son, and you will stray
> from the words of knowledge.[10]

> Reproofs of instruction are the way of life.[11]

> Pride only breeds quarrels, but wisdom is found in those
> who take advice.[12]

Divine warnings. All inspired by God and tested by time. They're yours to do with as you wish. They are red lights on your dashboard. Heed them and safety is yours to enjoy. Ignore them and I'll be looking for you on the side of the road.

CHAPTER 24

FATHER'S DAY:
A TRIBUTE

Today is Father's Day. A day of cologne. A day of hugs, new neckties, long-distance telephone calls, and Hallmark cards.

Today is my first Father's Day without a father. For thirty-one years I had one. I had one of the best. But now he's gone. He's buried under an oak tree in a west Texas cemetery. Even though he's gone, his presence is very near—especially today.

It seems strange that he isn't here. I guess that's because he was never gone. He was always close by. Always available. Always present. His words were nothing novel. His achievements, though admirable, were nothing extraordinary.

But his presence was.

Like a warm fireplace in a large house, he was a source of comfort. Like a sturdy porch swing or a big-branched elm in the backyard, he could always be found and leaned upon.

During the turbulent years of my adolescence, Dad was one part of my life that was predictable. Girlfriends came and girlfriends went, but Dad was there.

Football season turned into baseball season and turned into football season again and Dad was always there. Summer vacation, Homecoming dates, algebra, first car, driveway basketball—they all had one thing in common: his presence.

And because he was there life went smoothly. The car always ran, the bills got paid, and the lawn stayed mowed. Because he was there the laughter was fresh and the future was secure. Because he was there my growing up was what God intended growing up to be; a storybook scamper through the magic and mystery of the world.

Because he was there we kids never worried about things like income tax, savings accounts, monthly bills or mortgages. Those were the things on Daddy's desk.

We have lots of family pictures without him. Not because he wasn't there, but because he was always behind the camera.

He made the decisions, broke up the fights, chuckled at Archie Bunker, read the paper every evening, and fixed breakfast on Sundays. He didn't do anything unusual. He only did what dads are supposed to do—be there.

He taught me how to shave and how to pray. He helped me memorize verses for Sunday school and taught me that wrong should be punished and that rightness has its own reward. He modeled the importance of getting up early and of staying out of debt. His life expressed the elusive balance between ambition and self-acceptance.

He comes to mind often. When I smell "Old Spice" after-shave, I think of him. When I see a bass boat I see his face. And occasionally, not too often, but occasionally when I hear a good joke (the kind Red Skelton would tell), I hear him chuckle. He had a copyright chuckle that always came with a wide grin and arched eyebrows.

Daddy never said a word to me about sex nor told me his life story. But I knew that if I ever wanted to know, he would tell me. All I had to do was ask. And I knew if I ever needed him, he'd be there.

Like a warm fireplace.

Maybe that's why this Father's Day is a bit chilly. The fire has gone out. The winds of age swallowed the last splendid flame, leaving only golden embers. But there is a strange thing about those embers, stir them a bit and a flame will dance. It will dance only briefly, but it will dance. And it will knock just enough chill out of the air to remind me that he is still—in a special way—very present.

CHAPTER 25

FAMILY SEDANS OF THE FAITH

For an extraordinary pitcher he performed few extraordinary feats. Though a veteran of twenty-one seasons, in only one did he win more than twenty games. He never pitched a no-hitter and only once did he lead the league in any category (2.21 ERA, 1980).

Yet on June 21, 1986, Don Sutton rubbed pitching elbows with the true legends of baseball by becoming the thirtieth pitcher to win 300 games.

His analysis of his success is worth noting.

"A grinder and a mechanic" is what he calls himself. "I never considered myself flamboyant or exceptional. But all my life I've found a way to get the job done."

And get it done he did. Through two decades, six presidential terms, and four trades, he consistently did what pitchers are supposed to do: win games. With tunnel-vision devotion, he spent twenty-one seasons redefining greatness.

He has been called the "family sedan" of baseball's men on the mound.[1] The connotation is accurate. He certainly boasted none of the Ferrari style of a Denny McClane nor the Mercedes sparkle of a Sandy Koufax, but after they and their types were parked in museums or garages, Don Sutton was still there.

He reminds us of a quality that is a common denominator in any form of greatness—reliability.

It's the bread and butter characteristic of achievement. It's the shared ingredient behind retirement pens, Hall of Fame awards, and golden anniversaries. It is the quality that produces not momentary heroics but monumental lives.

The Bible has its share of family sedans. Consistent and predictable, these saints were spurred by a gut-level conviction that they had been called by no one less than God himself. As a result, their work wasn't affected by moods, cloudy days, or rocky trails. Their performance graph didn't rise and fall with roller-coaster irregularity. They weren't addicted to accolades or applause nor deterred by grumpy bosses or empty wallets. Rather than strive to be spectacular, they aspired to be accountable and dependable. And since their loyalty was not determined by their comfort, they were just as faithful in dark prisons as they were in spotlighted pulpits.

Reliable servants. They're the binding of the Bible. Their acts are rarely recited and their names are seldom mentioned. Yet were it not for their loyal devotion to God, many great events never would have occurred. Here are some examples.

Andrew wasn't a keynoter at the Pentecost crusade. He probably wasn't on the podium, on the schedule, or even on the planning committee. But if he hadn't been on his toes some years earlier, Peter the powerful preacher might have been nothing more than Peter the impetuous fish-catcher. Andrew, considering he was an apostle, is mentioned a surprisingly small number of times. Yet every time he is mentioned he's doing the same thing: introducing somebody to Jesus. No lights, no pulpits, no reviews, but not a bad epitaph.[2]

Epaphroditus would be on this list. "Epaphro-what-us?" you say. Just ask the apostle Paul. He'll give you the correct pronunciation. He'll also give quite a character reference.[3] To describe this fellow with the five-syllable name Paul used more succinct words like *brother, fellow worker, fellow soldier,* and *messenger.* You don't earn eulogies like these from appearing at an occasional youth rally or showing up at church picnics. These are compliments earned over years and tears. But Paul's finest praise of Epaphroditus was expressed in these words, "he almost died for the gospel." You can bet that Paul, who knew what it meant to die for a cause, didn't take sacrifice for granted. After writing the phrase, he must have leaned back against his prison wall and smiled at the mental picture of his old trail-buddy. Epaphroditus. The only thing longer than his name was his staying power.

Her hair is gray. Her skin is wrinkled. Perhaps her hand trembles as she touches the infant's face. But there is nothing senile about her words. "This is he. The Messiah." Anna should know. She'd been praying and fasting for this day for eight decades. Faithful servants have a way of knowing answered prayer when they see it, and a way of not giving up when they don't.

Re-liable. *Liable* means responsible. *Re* means over and over again.

I'm wondering if this book has found it's way into the hands of some contemporary saints of reliability. If such is the case I can't resist the chance to say two things.

The first?

Thank you.

Thank you senior saints for a generation of prayer and forest clearing.

Thank you teachers for the countless Sunday school lessons, prepared and delivered with tenderness.

Thank you missionaries for your bravery in sharing the timeless truth in a foreign tongue.

Thank you preachers. You thought we weren't listening, but we were. And your stubborn sowing of God's seed is bearing fruit you may never see this side of the great harvest.

Thanks to all of you who practice on Monday what you hear on Sunday. You spent selfless hours with orphans, at typewriters, in board meetings, on knees, in hospital wards, away from families, and on assembly lines. It is upon the back of your fidelity that the gospel rides.

Thank you for being the family sedans of society. You can be called on cold mornings and you'll deliver the goods. You can be sent over rough terrain and you'll make it on time. You can go miles without the pampering of a good polish or the luxury of a tune-up and you never complain. You get the job done.

I said I had two things to say. What is the second?

Keep pitching. Your Hall of Fame award is just around the corner.

CHAPTER 26

INSENSITIVE SLURS

Insensitivity makes a wound that heals slowly. If someone hurts your feelings intentionally you know how to react. You know the source of the pain. But if someone accidentally bruises your soul, it's difficult to know how to respond.

Someone at work criticizes the new boss who also happens to be your dear friend. "Oh, I'm sorry—I forgot the two of you were so close."

A joke is told at a party about overweight people. You're overweight. You hear the joke. You smile politely while your heart sinks.

What was intended to be a reprimand for a decision or action becomes a personal attack. "You have a history of poor decisions, John."

Someone chooses to wash your dirty laundry in public. "Sue, is it true that you and Jim are separated?"

Insensitive comments. Thoughts that should have remained thoughts. Feelings which had no business being expressed. Opinions carelessly tossed like a grenade into a crowd.

And if you were to tell the one who threw these thoughtless darts about the pain they caused, his response would be "Oh, but I had no intention...I didn't realize you were so sensitive!" or "I forgot you were here."

In a way, the words are comforting, until you stop to think about them (which is not recommended). For when you start to think about insensitive slurs, you realize they come from an infamous family whose father has bred generations of pain. His name? Egotism. His children? Three sisters: Disregard, disrespect, and disappointment.

These three witches have combined to poison countless relationships and break innumerable hearts. Listed among their weapons are Satan's cruelest artillery: gossip, accusations, resentment, impatience, and on and on. And listed under the tide of *subterfuge* is this poison of insensitivity.

It's called subterfuge because it's so subtle. Just a slip of the tongue. Just a blank of memory. No one is at fault. No harm done.

Perhaps. And, perhaps not. For as the innocent attackers go on their way excusing themselves for things done without hurtful intention, a wounded soul is left in the dust, utterly confused. "If no one intended to hurt me, then why do I hurt so badly?"

God's Word has strong medicine for those who carelessly wag their tongues.

> The tongue also is a fire, a world of evil among the parts of the body. It corrupts the whole person, sets the whole course of his life on fire, and is itself set on fire by hell.[1]

> He who guards his mouth and his tongue keeps himself from calamity.[2]

> He who guards his lips guards his soul, but he who speaks rashly will come to ruin.[3]

> When words are many, sin is not absent, but he who holds his tongue is wise.[4]

The message is clear: He who dares to call himself God's ambassador is not afforded the luxury of idle words. Excuses such as "I didn't know you were here" or "I didn't realize this was so touchy" are shallow when they come from those who claim to be followers and imitators of the Great Physician. We have an added responsibility to guard our tongues.

These practical steps will purge careless words from your talk.

1. Never tell jokes that slander.
2. Never criticize in public unless you: have already expressed your disappointment with the other person in private, have

already taken someone with you to discuss the grievance with the person, and are absolutely convinced that public reprimand is necessary and will be helpful.

3. Never say anything about anyone in their absence that you wouldn't say in their presence.

Insensitive slurs may be accidental, but they are not excusable.

CHAPTER 27

A SONG
IN THE DARK

On any other day, I probably wouldn't have stopped. Like the majority of people on the busy avenue, I would hardly have noticed him standing there. But the very thing on my mind was the very reason he was there, so I stopped.

I'd just spent a portion of the morning preparing a lesson out of the ninth chapter of John, the chapter that contains the story about the man blind from birth. I'd finished lunch and was returning to my office when I saw him. He was singing. An aluminum cane was in his left hand; his right hand was extended and open, awaiting donations. He was blind.

After walking past him about five steps, I stopped and mumbled something to myself about the epitome of hypocrisy and went back in his direction. I put some change in his hand. "Thank you," he said and then offered me a common Brazilian salutation, "and may you have health." Ironic wish.

Once again I started on my way. Once again the morning study of John 9 stopped me. "Jesus saw a man, blind from birth." I paused and pondered. If Jesus were here he would *see* this man. I wasn't sure what that meant. But I was sure I hadn't done it. So I turned around again.

As if the giving of a donation entitled me to do so, I stopped beside a nearby car and observed. I challenged myself to see him. I would stay here until I saw more than a sightless indigent on a busy thoroughfare in downtown Rio de Janeiro.

I watched him sing. Some beggars grovel in a corner cultivating pity. Others unashamedly lay their children on blankets in the middle of the sidewalk thinking that only the hardest of hearts would ignore a dirty, naked infant asking for bread.

But this man did none of that. He stood. He stood tall. And he sang. Loudly. Even proudly. All of us had more reason to sing than he, but he was the one singing. Mainly, he sang folk songs. Once I thought he was singing a hymn, though I wasn't sure.

His husky voice was out of place amid the buzz of commerce. Like a small sparrow who found his way into a noisy factory, or a lost fawn on an interstate, his singing conjured an awkward marriage between progress and simplicity.

The passersby had various reactions. Some were curious and gazed unabashedly. Others were uncomfortable. They were quick to duck their heads or walk in a wider circle. "No reminders of harshness today, please." Most, however, hardly noticed him. Their thoughts were occupied, their agendas were full and he was…well, he was a blind beggar.

I was thankful he couldn't see the way they looked at him.

After a few minutes I went up to him again. "Have you had any lunch?" I asked. He stopped singing. He turned his head toward the sound of my voice and directed his face somewhere past my ear. His eye sockets were empty. He said he was hungry. I went to a nearby restaurant and bought him a sandwich and something cold to drink.

When I came back he was still singing and his hands were still empty. He was grateful for the food. We sat down on a nearby bench. Between bites he told me about himself. Twenty-eight years old. Single. Lives with his parents and seven brothers. "Were you born blind?"

"No, when I was young I had an accident." He didn't volunteer details and I didn't have the gall to request them.

Though we were almost the same age, we were light years apart. My three decades had been a summer vacation of family excursions, Sunday school, debate teams, football, and a search for the Mighty One. Growing up blind in the Third World surely offered none of these. My daily concern now involved people, thoughts, concepts, and communication. His day was stitched with concerns of survival: coins, handouts, and food. I'd go home to a nice apartment, a hot meal, and a good wife. I hated to think of the home he would encounter. I'd seen enough overcrowded huts on the hills of Rio to make a reasonable guess. And his reception...would there be anyone to make him feel special when he got home?

I came whisker-close to asking him, "Does it make you mad that I'm not you?" "Do you ever lie awake at night wondering why the hand you were dealt was so different from the one given a million or so others born thirty years ago?"

I wore a shirt and tie and some new shoes. His shoes had holes and his coat was oversized and bulky. His pants gaped open from a rip in the knee.

And still he sang. Though a sightless, penniless hobo, he still found a song and sang it courageously. (I wondered which room in his heart that song came from.)

At worst, I figured, he sang from desperation. His song was all he had. Even when no one gave any coins, he still had his song. Yet he seemed too peaceful to be singing out of self-preservation.

Or perhaps he sang from ignorance. Maybe he didn't know what he never had.

No, I decided the motivation that fit his demeanor was the one you'd least expect. He was singing from contentment. Somehow this eyeless pauper had discovered a candle called satisfaction and it glowed in his dark world. Someone had told him, or maybe he'd told himself, that tomorrow's joy is fathered by today's acceptance. Acceptance of what, at least for the moment, you cannot alter.

I looked up at the Niagara of faces that flowed past us. Grim. Professional. Some determined. Some disguised. But none were singing, not even silently. What if each face were a billboard that announced the true state of its owner's heart? How many would say "Desperate! Business on the rocks!" or "Broken: In Need of Repair," or "Faithless, Frantic, and Fearful"? Quite a few.

The irony was painfully amusing. This blind man could be the most peaceful fellow on the street. No diploma, no awards, and no future—at least in the aggressive sense of the word. But I wondered how many in that urban stampede would trade their boardrooms and blue suits in a second for a chance to drink at this young man's well.

"Faith is the bird that sings while it is yet dark."

Before I helped my friend back to his position on the street, I tried to verbalize my empathy. "Life is hard, isn't it?" A slight smile. He again turned his face toward the direction of my voice and started to respond, then paused and said, "I'd better get back to work."

For almost a block, I could hear him singing. And in my mind's eye I could still see him. But the man I now saw was a different one than the one to whom I'd given a few coins. Though the man I now saw was still sightless, he was remarkably insightful. And though I was the one with eyes, it was he who gave me a new vision.

CHAPTER 28

IN THE MUD OF JABBOK

H e was the riverboat gambler of the patriarchs. A master of sleight of hand and fancy footwork. He had gained a seamy reputation of getting what he wanted by hook or crook—or both.

Twice he dealt hidden cards to his dull-witted brother Esau in order to climb the family tree. He once pulled the wool over the eyes of his own father, a trick especially dirty since his father's eyes were rather dim, and the wool he pulled insured him a gift he would never have received otherwise.

He later conned his father-in-law out of his best livestock and, when no one was looking, he took the kids and the cattle and skedaddled.

Yes, Jacob had a salty reputation, deservedly so. For him the ends always justified the means. His cleverness was outranked only by his audacity. His conscience was calloused just enough to let him sleep and his feet were just fast enough to keep him one step ahead of the consequences.

That is, until he reached a river called Jabbok.[1] At Jabbok his own cunning caught up with him.

Jacob was camped near the river Jabbok when word reached him that big, hairy Esau was coming to see him. It had been twenty years since Jacob had tricked his brother. More than enough time, Jacob realized, for Esau to stir up a boiling pot of revenge. Jacob was in trouble. This time he had no more tricks up his sleeve. He was finally forced to face up to himself and to God.

To Jacob's credit, he didn't run away from the problem. One has to wonder why. Maybe he was sick of running. Or maybe he was tired of looking at the shady character he saw every morning in the mirror. Or maybe he simply knew that he'd dealt from the bottom of the deck one too many times. Whatever the motivation, it was enough to cause him to come out of the shadows, cross Jabbok Creek alone, and face the facts.

The word *Jabbok* in Hebrew means "wrestle," and wrestle is what Jacob did. He wrestled with his past: all the white lies, scheming, and scandalizing. He wrestled with his situation: a spider trapped in his own web of deceit and craftiness. But more than anything, he wrestled with God.

He wrestled with the same God who had descended the ladder at Bethel to assure Jacob he wasn't alone (although he deserved to be). He met the same God who had earlier guaranteed Jacob that he would never break his promise (though one could hardly fault God if he did). He confronted the same God who had reminded Jacob that the land prepared for him was still his. (Proof again that God blesses us *in spite* of our lives and not *because of* our lives.)

Jacob wrestled with God the entire night. On the banks of Jabbok he rolled in the mud of his mistakes. He met God face to face, sick of his past and in desperate need of a fresh start. And because Jacob wanted it so badly, God honored his determination. God gave him a new name and a new promise. But he also gave a wrenched hip as a reminder of that mysterious night at the river.

Jacob wasn't the only man in the Bible to wrestle with self and God because of past antics. David did after his rendezvous with Bathsheba. Samson wrestled, blind and bald after Delilah's seduction. Elijah was at his own Jabbok when he heard the "still, small voice." Peter wrestled with his guilt with echoes of a crowing cock still ringing in his ears.

And I imagine that most of us have spent some time on the river banks as well. Our scandalous deeds have a way of finding us. Want some examples? Consider these scenes.

The unfaithful husband standing at the table with a note from his wife in his hands, "I couldn't take it anymore. I've taken the kids with me."

The twenty-year-old single in the doctor's office. The words are still fresh on her mind, "The test was positive. You are pregnant."

The businessman squirming in the IRS office. "Your audit shows that you took some loopholes that weren't yours to take."

The red-faced student who got caught red-handed copying the test answers of someone else. "We'll have to notify your parents."

All of us at one time or another come face to face with our past. And it's always an awkward encounter. When our sins catch up with us we can do one of two things: run or wrestle.

Many choose to run. They brush it off with a shrug of rationalization. "I was a victim of circumstances." Or, "It was his fault." Or, "There are many who do worse things." The problem with this escape is that it's no escape at all. It's only a shallow camouflage. No matter how many layers of make-up you put over a black eye, underneath it is still black. And down deep it still hurts.

Jacob finally figured that out. As a result, his example is one worthy of imitation. The best way to deal with our past is to hitch up our pants, roll up our sleeves, and face it head on. No more buck-passing or scapegoating. No more glossing over or covering up. No more games. We need a confrontation with our Master.

We too should cross the creek alone and struggle with God over ourselves. We too should stand eyeball to eyeball with him and be reminded that left alone we fail. We too should unmask our stained hearts and grimy souls and be honest with the One who knows our most secret sins.

The result could be refreshing. We know it was for Jacob. After his encounter with God, Jacob was a new man. He crossed the river in the dawn of a new day and faced Esau with newly found courage.

Each step he took, however, was a painful one. His stiff hip was a reminder of the lesson he had learned at Jabbok: Shady dealings bring pain. Mark it down: Play today and tomorrow you'll pay.

And for you who wonder if you've played too long to change, take courage from Jacob's legacy. No man is too bad for God. To transform a riverboat gambler into a man of faith would be no easy task. But for God, it was all in a night's work.

CHAPTER 29

A LITTLE BIT
OF HANGIN'

"Lord...let me know how fleeting my life is!"
PSALM 39:4

Abraham Lincoln once listened to the pleas of the mother of a soldier who'd been sentenced to hang for treason. She begged the president to grant a pardon. Lincoln agreed. Yet, he's reported to have left the lady with the following words: "Still, I wish we could teach him a lesson. I wish we could give him just a little bit of hangin'."

I think I know what the old rail-splitter had in mind. Yesterday, I got a little bit of hangin'.

We were having Sunday lunch at the home of a fellow missionary family. It was after the meal, and I was in the kitchen while Denalyn and our friends, Paul and Debbie, were talking in the living room. Their three-year-old daughter Beth Ann was playing with our two-year-old Jenna in the front yard. All of a sudden Beth Ann rushed in with a look of panic on her face. "Jenna is in the pool!"

Paul was the first to arrive at the poolside. He went straight into the water. Denalyn was next to arrive. By the time I arrived, Paul had lifted her up out of the water to the extended hands of her mother. Jenna was simultaneously choking, crying, and coughing. She vomited a bellyful of water. I held her as she cried. Denalyn began to weep. I began to sweat.

For the rest of the day I couldn't hold her enough, nor could we thank little Beth Ann enough (we took her out for ice cream). I still can't thank God enough.

It was only a matter of minutes, maybe seconds. We almost lost her. The thought was numbing and convicting.

It was a little bit of hangin'.

The stool was kicked out from under my feet and the rope jerked around my neck just long enough to remind me of what really matters. It was a divine slap, a gracious knock on the head, a severe mercy. Because of it I came face to face with one of the underground's slyest agents—the agent of familiarity.

His commission from the black throne room is clear, and fatal: "Take nothing from your victim; cause him only to take everything for granted."

He'd been on my trail for years and I never knew it. But I know it now. I've come to recognize his tactics and detect his presence. And I'm doing my best to keep him out. His aim is deadly. His goal is nothing less than to take what is most precious to us and make it appear most common.

To say that this agent of familiarity breeds contempt is to let him off easy. Contempt is just one of his offspring. He also sires broken hearts, wasted hours, and an insatiable desire for more. He's an expert in robbing the sparkle and replacing it with the drab. He invented the yawn and put the hum in the humdrum. And his strategy is deceptive.

He won't steal your salvation; he'll just make you forget what it was like to be lost. You'll grow accustomed to prayer and thereby not pray. Worship will become commonplace and study optional. With the passing of time he'll infiltrate your heart with boredom and cover the cross with dust so you'll be "safely" out of reach of change. Score one for the agent of familiarity.

Nor will he steal your home from you; he'll do something far worse. He'll paint it with a familiar coat of drabness.

He'll replace evening gowns with bathrobes, nights on the town with evenings in the recliner, and romance with routine. He'll scatter the dust of yesterday over the wedding pictures in the hallway until they become a memory of another couple in another time.

He won't take your children, he'll just make you too busy to notice them. His whispers to procrastinate are seductive. There is always next summer to coach the team, next month to go to the lake, and next week to teach Johnny how to pray. He'll make you forget that the faces around your table will soon be at tables of their own. Hence, books will go unread, games will go unplayed, hearts will go unnurtured, and opportunities will go ignored. All because the poison of the ordinary has deadened your senses to the magic of the moment.

Before you know it, the little face that brought tears to your eyes in the delivery room has become—perish the thought—common. A common kid sitting in the back seat of your van as you whiz down the fast lane of life. Unless something changes, unless someone wakes you up, that common kid will become a common stranger.

A little bit of hangin' might do us all a bit of good.

On a shelf above my desk is a picture of two little girls. They're holding hands and standing in front of a swimming pool, the same pool from which the younger of the two had been pulled only minutes before. I put the picture where I would see it daily so I would remember what God doesn't want me to forget.

And you can bet this time I'm going to remember. I don't want any more hangin'. Not even a little bit.

CHAPTER 30

CARMELITA

The hot air hung thickly in the small cemetery chapel. Those who had fans used them to stir the stillness. It was crowded. The few chairs that had been set out were quickly taken. I found an empty corner off to one side and stood quietly, observing my first Brazilian funeral.

On a stand in the midst of the chapel rested the coffin and body of a woman who had been killed the day before in a car accident. Her name was Dona Neusa. I knew her because she was the mother of one of our first converts, Cesar Coutinho. Beside the casket stood Cesar, his sister, other relatives, and someone very special by the name of Carmelita.

She was a tall woman with dark, almost black skin. On this day her dress was simple and her face solemn. She stared earnestly at the casket with deep-set brown eyes. There was something noble about the way she stood beside the body. She didn't weep openly as did the rest. Nor did she seek comfort from the other mourners. She just stood there, curiously quiet.

The night before, I had accompanied Cesar on the delicate task of telling Carmelita that Dona Neusa had been killed. As we drove, he explained to me how Carmelita had been adopted into their family.

Over twenty years earlier, Cesar's family had visited a small town in the interior of Brazil. There they encountered Carmelita, a seven-year-old orphan living with poverty-stricken relatives. Her mother had been a prostitute. She never knew her father. Upon seeing the child, Dona Neusa was touched. She knew that unless someone intervened, little Carmelita was doomed to a life with no love or attention. Because of

Dona Neusa's compassion, Cesar and his family returned home with a new family member.

As I stood in the funeral chapel and looked at Carmelita's face, I tried to imagine the emotions she was feeling. How her life had changed. I wondered if her mind was reliving that childhood memory of climbing into a car and driving away with a strange family. One moment she had been without love, a home, or a future; the next moment she had all three.

My thoughts were interrupted by the noise of shuffling feet. The funeral was over and people were leaving the chapel for the burial. Because of my position in the extreme corner of the building, I was the last to leave. Or at least so I thought. As I was walking out I heard a soft voice behind me. I turned and saw Carmelita weeping silently at the side of the coffin. Moved, I stood in the chapel doorway and witnessed this touching *adieu*. Carmelita was alone for the last time with her adopted mother. There was an earnestness in her eyes. It was as if she had one final task to perform. She didn't wail, nor did she scream with grief. She simply leaned over the casket and caressed it tenderly as if it were the face of her mother. With silent teardrops splashing on the polished wood she said repeatedly, *"Obrigada, obrigada"* ("Thank you, thank you").

A final farewell of gratitude.

Driving home that day, I thought how we, in many ways, are like Carmelita. We too were frightened orphans. We too were without tenderness or acceptance. And we too were rescued by a compassionate visitor, a generous parent who offered us a home and a name.

Our response should be exactly that of Carmelita, a stirring response of heartfelt gratitude for our deliverance. When no one else would even give us the time of day the Son of God gave us the time of our life!

We, too, should stand in the quiet company of him who saved us, and weep tears of gratitude and offer words of thankfulness. For it is not our bodies that have been rescued, but our souls.

CHAPTER 31

SEEING
THE SUMMIT

T his book was written at night. Not at dusk, nor in the evening, but at night. Past the bedtime hours. After the guests left. When the house was silent. While my wife was sleeping, I would slip into my storage closet converted into an office, greet my midnight mistress (my computer), and write. With the unceasing din of the city streets below and the soothing hum of the floor fan at my side, I enjoyed a nightly encounter with Light.

I'm not nocturnal by nature. Many nights a war was waged between my drowsiness and creativity. No, I'm not a late-nighter. But I'm a father and I'm a missionary and I found that the demands from those two tasks subsided about the hour when most people say "Good night." (I tried the early morning hours, which for some reason seemed more righteous— but the tow truck I needed to pull me out of bed couldn't make it up the stairs.)

Tonight appears to be my last rendezvous with this manuscript. *God Came Near* has gone through the necessary stages of feeding and grooming and is almost ready to be taken to market. Which, as you might expect, is a reason both for rejoicing and sadness. I'll miss this companion of the night. I don't mind telling you that more than once the impact of my late-hour ponderings took me out of my swivel chair and put me on my knees in thankfulness. We serve a wonderful God!

I recently read an insightful story that would serve as a good reminder for us both as we prepare to part ways. The story is about a group of climbers who set out to scale a large mountain in Europe. The view boasted a breathtaking peak of snowcapped rocks. On clear days the crested point reigned as king on the horizon. Its white tip jutted into the blue sky inviting admiration and offering inspiration.

On days like this the hikers made the greatest progress. The peak stood above them like a compelling goal. Eyes were called upward. The walk was brisk. The cooperation was unselfish. Though many, they climbed as one, all looking to the same summit.

Yet on some days the peak of the mountain was hidden from view. The cloud covering would eclipse the crisp blueness with a drab, gray ceiling and block the vision of the mountaintop. On these days the climb became arduous. Eyes were downward and thoughts inward. The goal was forgotten. Tempers were short. Weariness was an uninvited companion. Complaints stung like thorns on the trail.

We're like that, aren't we? As long as we can see our dream, as long as our goal is within eyesight, there is no mountain we can't climb or summit we can't scale. But take away our vision, block our view of the trail's end, and the result is as discouraging as the journey.

Think about it. Hide the Nazarene who calls to us from the mountaintop and see what happens.

Listen to the groans of the climbers as they stop and sit by the side of the path. Why continue if there is no relief in sight? Pilgrims with no vision of the promised land become proprietors of their own land. They set up camp. They exchange hiking boots for loafers and trade in their staff for a new recliner.

Instead of looking upward at him, they look inward at themselves and outward at each other. The result? Cabin fever. Quarreling families. Restless leaders. Fence-building. Staked-off territory. No trespassing! signs are hung on hearts and homes. Spats turn into fights as myopic groups turn to glare at each other's weaknesses instead of turning to worship their common Strength.

Mark it down. We are what we see. If we see only ourselves, our tombstones will have the same epitaph Paul used to describe enemies of Christ: "Their god is their own appetite, they glory in their shame, and this world is the limit of their horizon."[1] Humans were never meant to dwell in the stale fog of the lowlands with no vision of their Creator.

That's why God came near. To be seen.

And that's why those who saw him were never the same. "We saw his glory" exclaimed one follower.[2] "We were eyewitnesses of his majesty," whispered a martyr.[3] They saw the peak. They breathed the fresh air of the high country. They caught a glimpse of the pinnacle. And they refused to quit climbing until they reached the top. They wanted to see Jesus.

I began this book with some definitions: Christianity, in its purest form, is nothing more than seeing Jesus. Christian service, in its purest form, is nothing more than imitating him who we see. To see His Majesty and to imitate him, that is the sum of Christianity.

This is why those who see him today are never the same again. Remember Bob Edens? He's the one I told you about in the introduction who lived fifty-one years without seeing anything at all until complicated surgery gave him eyesight. Something else he said is worth noting.

"Grass was something I had to get used to…I always thought it was just fuzz. But to see each individual green stalk, and to see the hair on my arm growing like trees, and birds flying through the air…it's like starting a whole new life."

Getting vision can be like that. Especially getting a vision of your Maker. It can be like starting a whole new life. It can be like a new birth. In fact, the One who inspired this book said that new beginnings and good eyesight are inseparable. "Unless a man is born again, he cannot see the kingdom of God."[4]

God came near. If he is who he says he is, there is no truth more worthy of your time.

Think about that. Now, if you don't mind, I think I'll get some sleep.

STUDY
GUIDE

THE ARRIVAL

1. *God goes to those who have time to hear him—so on this cloudless night he went to simple shepherds.*

> A. If the Messiah had been born in our time, to what group do you think the angels would have made the announcement? Who do you suppose would have taken time to listen?

> B. Read Luke 2:8–20 to see the shepherds' reaction to the announcement. How did they respond? Why do you think God chose them to receive the good news?

> C. Read Luke 7:18–30 to see how others reacted to the news that the Messiah had come. How did Jesus respond when they asked if he was the Messiah? What was the response of the crowds? What was the response of the Pharisees and the experts in the law? Why do you think each group responded as it did?

> D. In what ways do you hear God? How often do you set aside time just to listen to him? When does God "have your ear"?

2. *Those who missed His Majesty's arrival that night missed it not because of evil acts or malice; no, they missed it because they simply weren't looking. Little has changed in the last two thousand years, has it?*

> A. How do you respond to Max's statement that little has changed in the last two thousand years? Do you think people are more or less receptive now? Why do you think so many people "miss his arrival"?

B. Read Proverbs 8:17 and John 14:21. What is promised to those who seek God?

C. According to Hebrews 11:6 and Hebrews 7:22–25, what is required of those who seek God? What is promised to them?

D. In what ways do you look for God? Where do you most often find him? In his Word? In prayer? In song? Manifested in his followers?

CHAPTER 2

"JUST A MOMENT..."

1. *There is something about keeping him [Jesus] divine that keeps him distant, packaged, predictable. But don't do it. For heaven's sake, don't. Let him be as human as he intended to be. Let him into the mire and muck of our world. For only if we let him in can he pull us out.*

A. Does it make you uncomfortable to think of Jesus in fully human terms? Why?

B. What does Max mean by "only if we let him in can he pull us out"? Do you agree? If Jesus had been able to save us without becoming human, how would that influence your attitude toward him as your Savior?

C. In the following passages, what aspects of Jesus seem very "human": Luke 24:36–43; Mark 4:35–40; John 11:1–36; Mark 14:32–40? Do those passages make him seem more real to you? How does the awareness of his humanity affect your relationship with him?

D. Read Psalm 103:8–18; Hebrews 2:14–18; and Hebrews 4:14–16. What reassurances do they give us that the Lord understands us and cares for us?

E. If you keep in mind both Jesus' divinity and humanity, how does that affect your ability to handle trials? How does it affect your ability to handle temptations? How does it affect your prayers?

2. *The world will see another instantaneous transformation. You see, in becoming man, God made it possible for man to see God. When Jesus went home he left the back door open.*

A. What is meant by "when Jesus went home he left the back door open"?

B. Read John 14:1–14. What kind of home is Jesus preparing? For whom?

C. Read Exodus 33:12–23 and 34:29–35. What happened when Moses asked to see God face to face? What effect did God's presence have on Moses?

D. According to Matthew 5:8; Hebrews 12:14; and Revelation 21:22–22:5, who will see the face of God?

E. What do you think of when you think about Jesus' return? What kind of emotions does it stir? Why? If you knew that Jesus' return was imminent, what priorities would you have? How would you spend your time?

CHAPTER 3

ABSURDITY IN THE FLESH

1. *After a nation of chosen ones had stripped him naked and ripped his incarnated flesh, he still died for them. And even today, after billions have chosen to prostitute themselves before the pimps of power, fame, and wealth, he still waits for them. It is inexplicable. It doesn't have a drop of logic nor a thread of rationality. And yet, it is that very irrationality that gives the gospel its greatest defense. For only God could love like that.*

A. Have you ever felt that the story of Jesus is absurd? Do you ever talk with people who challenge the authenticity of the story? How do you answer them?

B. How do these passages describe the love of God: Romans 5:6–8; Titus 3:3–8; Romans 8:13–17, 31–39?

C. According to 1 John 4:7–21, if we truly understand God's love for us, what is our response to him? What is our response to others? How does it affect our attitude toward the judgment day? What emotion cannot coexist with God's love in us?

D. When have you felt God's love most strongly? In what ways do you express God's love to others? How do you express your love to God?

2. *God became earth's mockery to save his children. How absurd to think that such nobility would go to such poverty to share such a treasure with such*

thankless souls. But he did. In fact, the only thing more absurd than the gift is our stubborn unwillingness to receive it.

A. How do we receive God's gift of salvation? Why do you think people don't accept God's gift of salvation?

B. Look up the following passages which describe people rejecting salvation: Luke 14:15–24; Romans 9:30–32; 1 Corinthians 1:18–31. According to these passages, what attitudes prevent people from accepting God's gift?

C. According to these passages, what are some of the attitudes and actions that characterize those who do accept God's salvation: Philippians 3:7–11; 2 Corinthians 7:10; Ephesians 2:8–9; James 1:19–27?

D. What attitude or action is the biggest challenge to your salvation?

CHAPTER 4

MARY'S PRAYER

1. *Rest well, tiny hands. For though you belong to a king you will touch no satin, own no gold. You will grasp no pen, guide no brush. No, your tiny hands are reserved for works more precious: to touch a leper's wounds, to wipe a widow's weary tear, to claw the ground of Gethsemane.*

A. What petitions to God do you make on behalf of your children?

B. Think about some of the ways Jesus used his hands here on earth. What do these passages tell us about his nature: Mark 1:40–42; Matthew 14:28–31; Matthew 9:18–26; Matthew 19:13–15; Mark 8:22–26; Luke 4:40; Luke 24:36–39? Was it necessary for Jesus to touch people in order to heal them? Why do you think he chose to touch them?

C. What instructions did Jesus leave us in Matthew 25:31–46 about showing compassion and helping those in need? What are the consequences of ignoring these commands?

D. Today it is easy to help people from a distance without ever having to deal with them face to face. What is lost without that personal contact? Why do we shy away from personal contact? What face to face involvement are you willing to have to carry out Jesus' commands?

2. *And little heart...holy heart...pumping the blood of life through the universe: How many times will we break you?*

A. When you sin and break the Lord's commands, what reaction do you see Jesus having? Anger? Disgust? Frustration? Disappointment? Condemnation? "I knew it all along"? Do you imagine it breaking his heart?

B. Look at these passages that describe God's mercy and compassion and forgiving spirit: Exodus 34:4–7; Isaiah 55:6–7; Jeremiah 9:23–24; Micah 7:18–19; Ephesians 2:1–10. How does God respond when we are truly repentant? What are the most revealing and significant words in each passage?

C. According to 2 Corinthians 1:3–7, in what way do we share in the sufferings of Christ? If we share in his sufferings, how do we also share in his comfort? How do we then share his comfort with others?

D. How would you chart the progression from being a sinner that breaks the heart of Jesus to being a person capable of ministering to others?

CHAPTER 5

LIMB-CLIMBER OR BRANCH-SITTER

1. *Joseph knew that the only thing worse than a venture into the unknown was the thought of denying his Master.*

    A. What difficulties lay ahead for Joseph by venturing with God into the unknown? What risks did he have to take?

    B. Although little is said about Joseph, note how he responded in each of these events: Matthew 1:18–24; Luke 2:21–24; Matthew 2:13–15; Matthew 2:19–23; Luke 2:41–48. How would you now characterize Joseph? How would you describe his belief in God?

    C. In what ways does God call us today to venture into the unknown?

2. *Have you been called to go out on a limb for God? You can bet it won't be easy. Limb-climbing has never been easy.*

    A. When have you felt that God was asking you to go out on a limb for him? How did you respond? What was the result?

    B. Look at some others that God called to go out on a limb. What risk did God ask these people to take: Abraham (Genesis 22:1–19); Moses (Exodus 3:1–4:18); Gideon (Judges 7); the widow at Zarephath (1 Kings 17:7–24); the rich young ruler (Luke 18:18–30)? How did each respond? How did God respond to their willingness or unwillingness to go out on a limb for his sake?

C. For you, which of these "limbs" would have required the greatest faith?

D. From these examples, what principles can you derive about God's response to our going out on a limb for him?

E. Is God calling you now to go out on a limb? How do you plan to respond?

CHAPTER 6

TWENTY-FIVE QUESTIONS FOR MARY

1. What have you wondered about Jesus' years growing up? What questions would you like to ask Mary?

2. What other questions would you like to ask Jesus?

3. Read John 1:1–14. How does John describe Jesus' existence prior to his being born to Mary?

4. Read Philippians 2:5–11. What was Jesus' attitude about coming to earth as a human? In what way should our attitude "be the same as that of Christ Jesus"?

5. If you could talk with one person from the Bible, other than Jesus, who would it be? Why? What questions would you ask?

6. Do you envision heaven as an opportunity to spend time talking with Jesus and Moses and Paul and people you have loved on earth? How does that make you feel about going to heaven?

CHAPTER 7

CHRISTMAS NIGHT

1. *The magical dust of Christmas glittered on the cheeks of humanity ever so briefly, reminding us of what is worth having and what we were intended to be.*

> A. What kind of Christmas traditions did you have growing up? What kind of traditions are you establishing in your own family?

> B. What are your priorities at Christmas time? Does Christmas time bring out the best or the worst in you?

> C. In reality, what are the only things that matter? What would these passages say are the most important things in life: Deuteronomy 10:12–13; Ecclesiastes 12:13–14; Matthew 22:34–40; James 1:25–27?

> D. What are your priorities for the next week? the next month? the next year?

2. *If he can do so much with such timid prayers lamely offered in December, how much more could he do if we thought of him every day?*

> A. Do we limit God's ability to act? If so, how?

> B. What images did Jesus use to describe the importance of commitment in these passages: Matthew 6:19–24; Mark 9:42–50; Matthew 13:1–23; Matthew 25:14–30?

C. What do the Scriptures say about consistency in and commitment to prayer? Read 1 Thessalonians 5:16–18; Ephesians 6:18; James 5:13–16; Luke 11:5–13; Luke 18:1–8.

D. In what way could you increase people's awareness of Christ throughout the year?

CHAPTER 8

OUT OF THE CARPENTRY SHOP

1. *You see, he didn't have to go. He had a choice. He could have stayed. He could have kept his mouth shut. He could have ignored the call or at least postponed it.*

A. Did Jesus have a choice? Do you think he made that choice once or numerous times? Do you think he ever doubted that humanity was worth the price he was going to pay?

B. What do the following passages reveal about not only Jesus' willingness but his determination to die for our sins: John 10:11–18; Matthew 26:36–54; John 18:4–11; Philippians 2:6–8; Hebrews 7:23–27?

C. On a piece of paper, in one column list everything Jesus chose to give up for your sake. In a second column, list everything he has asked you to give up for his sake.

2. *He saw your face aglow the hour you first knew him. He saw your face in shame the hour you first fell. The same face that looked back at you from this morning's mirror, looked at him. And it was enough to kill him. He left because of you.*

A. Is it difficult to conceive of Jesus seeing you and hearing you centuries before you were born? Is it difficult to realize that even now he sees and understands everything about you? How do you make Jesus a present reality in your life?

B. To better understand how well Jesus knows each of us, read the following passages: Psalm 139:1–18; Matthew 10:29–31; Hebrews 4:13. What insights do they give?

C. Read one of the Gospel accounts of Jesus' arrest, trial and crucifixion (e.g. Matthew 26:3–27:61). Can you imagine someone choosing to suffer that pain and abuse specifically for you? Can you imagine God choosing to do so? Why did God choose to die for you?

D. How would it alter your life if a friend died for you? How does it alter your life to realize that Jesus died for you?

CHAPTER 9

"Just Call
Me Jesus"

1. *There was not one person who considered him too holy, too divine, or too celestial to touch. There was not one person who was reluctant to approach him for fear of being rejected.*

A. For what reasons did people approach Jesus? What were people's reactions to him?

B. How did Jesus treat the outcasts of society? The moral outcasts (John 8:1–11)? The social outcasts (Mark 2:13–17)? The physical and spiritual outcasts (Matthew 8:1–4; Mark 5:1–20)?

C. How did Jesus treat those who rejected him? Judas (Matthew 26:47–50)? Peter (Mark 14:66–72; 16:1–7)? the rich, young ruler (Mark 10:17–27)? What is the most surprising element of each instance?

D. For whom were Jesus' harshest words reserved (Matthew 23; John 2:12–16)? Why did Jesus condemn them?

E. How Christlike and approachable arc you? to your children? your mate? your coworkers? strangers that you meet daily? those less fortunate than you? those who are "lower on the social ladder"? What could you do to make yourself more approachable?

2. *Remember. It is man who creates the distance. It is Jesus who builds the bridge.*

A. What causes people to move away from Jesus? Times of tragedy and difficulty? Times of success? Apathy? Why?

B. Based on the teachings in these passages, in what ways does Jesus build the bridge to us: Romans 8:5–17, 26; 1 John 5:14–15; John 5:24; Psalm 145:13b–20; Romans 5:6–8?

C. What images did Jesus use to show his concern for us? Look at these passages for some examples: Matthew 23:37; Luke 15:1–32; Isaiah 40:11. For you, which of these most powerfully illustrates his love for people?

D. Do you believe you are closer to or farther from Jesus than you were a year ago? In what ways would you like to move closer to him?

CHAPTER 10

WOMEN OF WINTER

1. *Those who scramble in at quitting time get the same wage as those who beat the morning whistle. I guess that's what makes grace, grace.*

A. Have you known of someone who came to Jesus in the "winter" of his or her life? Or someone who came with seemingly little to offer in Jesus' kingdom? What impact did this person have?

B. Look at the "rest of the story" of these three women in Luke 7:11–17; John 4:1–42; and Luke 8:43–47. What impact did they and these events have on the people around them?

C. What circumstances or characteristics in these people did Jesus use to further his kingdom?

D. What "winter people" do you know? What circumstances or characteristics in them could God use to touch their hearts and the hearts of those around them?

2. *No, no one would have blamed Jesus for ignoring the three women. To have turned his head would have been much easier, less controversial, and not nearly as risky. But God, who made them, couldn't do that. And we, who follow him, can't either.*

A. When are you tempted to turn your head rather than deal with a "risky" person? For you, what elements of society require more risk than you are willing to take? How willing is your church to get involved with the controversial elements of society?

B. After reading Matthew 10:28–42, how would you define "risk" from God's perspective? What are we to fear? What are we not to fear?

C. If you had only Luke 14:7–14 to go by, how would you describe Jesus' "social ladder"?

D. What three ingredients would be essential for your church to become more involved with the "winter people" of society?

CHAPTER 11

WHEN GOD SIGHED

1. *I'd thought of God as one who commands. I'd thought of God as one who weeps. I'd thought of God as one who calls forth the dead or created the universe with a command…but a God who sighs?*

    A. How do you most often picture God? Can you envision God sighing? What might prompt God to sigh? What emotions does that imply?

    B. Mark 7:34 describes it as a "deep sigh." Why do you think Jesus sighed? What lesson is there for us in Jesus' response?

    C. Compare this incident to the one in Mark 8:11–13. Why do you think Jesus sighed when the Pharisees questioned him? How might Jesus' feelings have differed from the previous incident?

    D. Read Romans 8:22–27 and 2 Corinthians 5:2–4 where Paul describes our groaning for heaven. What is conveyed by "groaning" in these passages?

    E. Would you describe yourself as a person who "groans" for heaven? Why or why not? What perspective on life does it imply?

2. *So, I found a place for the word [sigh]. You might think it strange, but I placed it beside the word* comfort, *for in an indirect way, God's pain is our comfort. And in the agony of Jesus lies our hope…. That holy sigh assures us*

that God still groans for his people. He groans for the day when all sighs will cease, when what was intended to be will be.

A. What does Max mean by "God's pain is our comfort"? In what way is that a true statement?

B. Read John 17:1–26. What was God's design for our relationship with Jesus? for our relationship with each other? What was "intended to be"? How does God comfort us until the "day that all sighs will cease"? Why is unity so important?

C. Spend some time reading psalms that speak of the comfort God provides, such as Psalm 23, Psalm 34, and Psalm 46. In what ways does God comfort us?

D. In what ways do you see believers unified? In what areas do we need to strive for greater unity?

CHAPTER 12

THE QUESTION FOR THE CANYON'S EDGE

1. *Only God can deal with our ultimate dilemma—death. And only the God of the Bible has dared to stand on the canyon's edge and offer an answer. He has to be God in the face of death. If not, he is not God anywhere.*

A. What does Max mean by "He has to be God in the face of death. If not, he is not God anywhere"? What is the answer to death that God offers? How did he offer the answer?

B. Read 1 Corinthians 15:12–28 and restate in your own words Paul's argument concerning death and resurrection.

C. How would you answer someone who questions that Jesus rose from the dead and that there is life after death?

2. *Do you believe that a young, penniless itinerant is larger than your death? Do you truly believe that death is nothing more than an entrance ramp to a new highway?*

A. Max describes death as an entrance ramp. What other helpful comparisons can you make to explain what death is like?

B. What insights do these passages give into the relationship of death to life: Luke 20:34–38; John 11:25–26; Romans 8:10–11?

C. What would you say to someone facing death that would help the person see God's answer?

CHAPTER 13

A TALE OF TWO TREES

1. *The struggle. The snake. The lie. The enticement. Heart torn, lured. Soul drawn to pleasure, to independence, to importance. Inner agony. Whose will?*

    A. Read Genesis 2:15–17 and 3:1–24. What temptations were present? What choices were made by Adam? by Eve? Whose will controlled the choices?

    B. To what extent are those same temptations still prevalent today? To which ones are we most susceptible?

    C. Based on Adam's and Eve's example, what makes us susceptible to temptation and to self-will?

2. *Once again the struggle. The snake. The enticement. Heart torn, lured. Once again the question, "Whose will?"*

    A. Read Matthew 26:1–75. What enticements were present at this struggle? for Judas? for Peter? for Jesus?

    B. To what extent are these temptations strong today?

    C. How did Jesus show submission to God's will at the Passover meal? in Gethsemane? at his arrest? before the high priest and the Sanhedrin?

    D. From Jesus' example, what principles can you deduce for resisting temptation and for submitting to God's will?

CHAPTER 14

NO ACCIDENT

1. *Jesus was born crucified. Whenever he became conscious of who he was, he also became conscious of what he had to do.*

   A. Do you ever wish you could know your future? What if that future held a painful death in an effort to save another person's life? Would you want to know ahead of time? Would you try to alter the course of events?

   B. As Jesus anticipates his imminent death in Matthew 16:21–23; Luke 9:51; Luke 13:31–32; and John 10:17–18, what attitudes about his coming death does he reveal? How did he respond to those who tried to alter his course?

   C. Is there a goal in your life that you pursue with single-minded devotion? Should there be such a goal? What would it be? How would it change your daily life to pursue it with total devotion?

2. *Had Jesus been forced to nail himself to the cross, he would have done it. For it was not the soldiers who killed him, nor the screams of the mob—it was his devotion to us.*

   A. How would you rank the following according to their responsibility for his death: Judas, the mob, the religious leaders, the Roman authorities, and the soldiers? Is there anyone else you would add to the list?

   B. According to these passages who was responsible for Jesus' death: Romans 5:8; Ephesians 2:1–5; 1 John 4:9–10?

C. According to Psalm 145:20; Ephesians 3:17–19; and John 14:23, what happens when we realize Jesus' devotion to us and respond with love for him?

D. As Jesus' death was an act of will on his part, how are our lives to be an act of will? What is the result when we don't make conscious choices to live for Jesus? What controls our lives?

CHAPTER 15

REDISCOVERING AMAZEMENT

1. *We wonder, with so many miraculous testimonies around us, how we could escape God. But somehow we do.... Or what is pathetically worse, we demand more. More signs. More proof. More hat tricks. As if God were some vaudeville magician we could summon for a dollar.*

A. Do you ever wish you could have witnessed the miracles Jesus performed on earth? Do you think it would increase your faith? Do you ever wish that God would perform a specific miracle for you now so that it would be easier to believe?

B. How did seeing Jesus' miracles affect people's faith? What different responses were there when Jesus raised Lazarus from the dead (John 11:38–53)?

C. Read these examples of people who asked for miracles: Matthew 12:38–39; Matthew 16:1–4; Acts 8:9–23. What was wrong with their motive in each case?

D. According to John 2:11; Acts 2:22; and John 20:30–31, what was God's purpose in miracles?

E. Upon what should our belief in Jesus be based?

2. *Would you like to see Jesus? Do you dare be an eyewitness of His Majesty? Then rediscover amazement.*

A. What event has most strongly impressed you with the majesty of God? For you, what setting most strongly reveals God's presence—the mountains, the ocean, a starry night, a rainbow?

B. Read some of the passages that describe God's miracles and majesty, such as Job 9:4–10; Job 38, 39; and Psalm 104. How do they affect your image of God? Based on these passages, what words would you use to describe God?

C. Read Job 42:1–6. What was Job's response to God's description of his power? In what way is your response similar? different?

CHAPTER 16

HOPE

1. *Our problem is not so much that God doesn't give us what we hope for as it is that we don't know the right thing for which to hope.*

    A. Give an instance in which God failed to answer a prayer, for which you were later grateful.

    B. Read 2 Samuel 7. What did David hope to do? What were his motives? What was God's answer to David? How did David respond to God's answer?

    C. Read the accounts in Matthew 20:20–28 and Mark 10:35–45 of the request made by James and John and their mother. What did they hope for? What appears to have been their motive? In what way were they hoping for the wrong thing?

    D. From these two examples and the others in the chapter, what principles can you determine about the things for which we should hope and pray? What should be our response when God answers us differently than we have hoped?

2. *Hope is not a granted wish or a favor performed; no, it is far greater than that. It is a zany, unpredictable dependence on a God who loves to surprise us out of our socks and be there in the flesh to see our reaction.*

    A. Have you ever been surprised by a far greater answer to your prayer than you could have anticipated? Give an example.

B. "Hope," as it is used in the New Testament, is not wishful thinking but confident expectation. It is not desire but dependence. Read the following passages substituting "confident expectation" for "hope" each place it appears: Romans 15:4; Titus 1:1–3; Titus 3:3–8; Hebrews 6:13–20; Hebrews 10:19–25 and Hebrews 11:1. How does that affect the impact of these verses? In your opinion, which verse does it make the strongest?

C. What do you "confidently expect" from God? Beyond what reason dictates, in what ways do you absolutely, unquestioningly depend on God?

CHAPTER 17

ETERNAL INSTANTS

1. *An eternal instant. A moment that reminds you of the treasures surrounding you. Your home. Your peace of mind. Your health.*

   A. Describe an "eternal instant" you experienced. What were the circumstances? What was the impact?

   B. According to the following passages, what are some of the treasures we have on earth: Psalm 127:3–5; Psalm 128:1–6; Proverbs 31:10–12; Proverbs 19:14?

   C. According to these examples, while Jesus was on earth, what did he do to stay focused on what was important: Matthew 14:22–23; Mark 1:35; Luke 5:15–16; Luke 9:18?

   D. In what way does our lifestyle work against "eternal instants"? What could we do to create more opportunities for these special moments? What could you do this week with your family—earthly or spiritual—that would remind you of what a blessing family is?

2. *Eternal instants remind us that love is still the greatest possession and the future is nothing to fear.*

   A. Do you agree that love is the greatest possession? If so, how would you justify that statement? If not, what is the greatest possession?

B.   What makes the future seem fearful? Do you expect the next ten years to be more difficult than the last ten? Do you look toward the turn of the century with anticipation or anxiety?

C. Read Psalm 103; 2 Timothy 2:11–13; and Hebrews 10:19–25. Who can face the future with confidence?
D. According to these passages, why can we feel secure about the future: Psalm 27:1–5; Psalm 121; Isaiah 54:10?

E.   How would you explain to a new Christian what is meant by "perfect love drives out fear" (1 John 4:18)?

CHAPTER 18

WHAT DO
YOU SEE?

1. *Seekers of popularity, power, and pleasure. The end result is the same: painful unfulfillment.*

    A. What examples can you give of people who have sought popularity, power, and pleasure only to find emptiness and pain?

    B. What did each of the following people seek: Absalom (2 Samuel 15:1–17; 2 Samuel 18:1–18); the Jewish leaders (John 12:37–50); Moses (Hebrews 11:23–28); the Corinthians (1 Corinthians 5:1–13; 6:9–20)? What was the result in each case?

    C. What wisdom does Proverbs offer in these passages regarding popularity, power, and pleasure: 21:17; 11:7; 13:20; 18:24; 19:6; 21:22; 25:6–7; 25:27?

    D. What proverb would you write regarding popularity, power, or pleasure? By contrast, what has brought you the most fulfillment in life?

2. *Destiny? Tomorrow? Truth? All are questions within the reach of the man who knows his source. It is in seeing Jesus that man sees his Source.*

    A. For the person who knows Jesus as his source, what are the answers to "What is my destiny?" "What does tomorrow hold?" and "What is truth?"

B. Read the following passages to see how Jesus answered these same questions: Destiny: Matthew 25:31–46; Tomorrow: Matthew 6:25–34; Truth: John 3:3–21; John 5:24–30; John 6:53–58; John 8:51; John 14:12. How would you restate his answer to each question?

C. What answers are there for the person who does not see Jesus as his source? Read John 3:18–20 and 1 John 5:10–12.

D. How would you direct someone to see Jesus as the source for life's answers?

CHAPTER 19

HE FORGOT

1. *For all the things he [God] does do, this is one thing he refuses to do. He refuses to keep a list of my wrongs.*

    A. What good can come from remembering our sins? At what point does it become harmful to remember our sins?

    B. The Bible uses several images to depict God's forgiveness of our sins. Which of these helps you most to visualize that God truly forgets: Psalm 103:12; Isaiah 1:18; Isaiah 43:25; Psalm 32:1; Isaiah 44:22?

    C. Read Psalm 32, which is a psalm of praise for God's forgiveness. What insights does it give into the effect of unconfessed sin? into God's response to the penitent heart?

    D. On a piece of paper, write down a sin that you have had difficulty forgiving in yourself. Then erase your writing or burn the paper. When you are tempted to agonize over that sin again, remember that it has been destroyed by God and by you.

2. *We are presumptuous not when we marvel at his grace, but when we reject it.*

    A. Why do you think people reject God's grace in forgiving sins? Why do people continue to feel guilty even after asking God's forgiveness?

B. Because we are clothed with Christ, how may we approach God's throne in prayer, according to these passages: Ephesians 3:8–12; Hebrews 4:14–16; Hebrews 10:19–23?

C. If we truly understand God's grace toward us, what is our natural response, according to Hebrews 10:24–25?

D. Based on the lesson, what do you want to remember better? What do you want to forget more easily?

CHAPTER 20

FACING THE FACTS

1. *Have you ever noticed the endless extremes to which a person will go to hide the realities of life?*

    A. What examples do you see of society's desire to hide or escape the realities of life, such as aging, death, and self? Do you see the trend increasing? If so, in what ways? What reality do you think people have the hardest time facing?

    B. What is God's perspective on aging, as seen in these passages: Job 12:12; Proverbs 16:31; Isaiah 46:4; Titus 2:3–5?

    C. What is God's perspective on us as his creation, as seen in these passages: Psalm 8:3–8; Psalm 139:1–18?

    D. How are the older members viewed in your church? What contributions do they make to the church? to the community? Are they isolated from the mainstream of the church, or are they active participants and leaders in the church's programs? What vital roles are they filling?

2. *Funerals, divorces, illnesses, and stays in the hospital—you can't lie about life at such times. Maybe that's why he's always present at such moments.*

    A. In the face of a serious illness or the death of a loved one, what was important to you? What was unimportant? What was comforting to you? What truths about life were especially clear?

B. What insight do these passages provide about God's perspective on death: Psalm 116:15; Romans 14:7–8; 1 Corinthians 15:50–58; Revelation 14:13?

C. What passage of Scripture is the most comforting to you when you consider the reality of death?

D. What would you want said about you at your funeral?

LIGHT OF THE... STORAGE CLOSET?

1. *"I'm not ready," the candle explained with pleading eyes. "I need more preparation."*

A. How much preparation is needed to be an effective "light" for Christ? When is too little preparation dangerous? In what way is excessive preparation dangerous? At what point does the desire for more preparation become an excuse for hiding one's light?

B. What can be learned from Acts 18:24–28; Hebrews 5:11–6:3; and James 1:22–25 about balancing preparation with action?

C. In what area are you best prepared to serve? In what ways could you use that preparation more fully?

2. *The last candle had a female voice, very pleasant to the ear. "I'd like to help," she explained, "but lighting the darkness is not my gift."*

A. How can we determine what our gifts are?

B. What do 1 Corinthians 12:1–11 and Romans 12:3–8 reveal about spiritual gifts?

C. What should our response be when we are asked to serve in an area that we don't consider our strength? Is it wisdom or selfishness not to serve in areas where we believe we aren't "gifted"? Why?

3. *"Where did you buy those candles anyway?" "Oh, they're church candles.
Remember the church that closed down across town? I bought them there."*

A. What is the meaning of Max's story about the candles? What
problems within churches is he pointing out? To what extent do
you see those problems surfacing among Christians?

CHAPTER 22

BLIND AMBITION

1. *Ambition is that grit in the soul which creates disenchantment with the ordinary and puts the dare into dreams.*

A. For you, what historical or contemporary person best exemplifies positive ambition—one who dared to dream?

B. Look at the following examples of people who dared to dream: Joshua (Numbers 13:1–14:9; 27:12–23); David (1 Samuel 17:1–54); and the Canaanite woman (Matthew 15:21–28). In each case, why do you believe they were successful in achieving their dreams?

C. What is your greatest ambition at this point in your life? What motivates that ambition?

2. *Blind ambition is a giant step away from God and one step closer to catastrophe.*

A. What modern examples can you give of blind ambition even within churches? How can we distinguish between a sincere desire to be a leader in the church and blind ambition?

B. There are several examples of men in the Bible who desired to "build" for the Lord—the men at Babel (Genesis 11:1–9); David (2 Samuel 7); and Peter (Matthew 17:1–8). In each case, why did God thwart their plans?

C. How does Psalm 127:1 relate to these examples?

D. What questions would you ask yourself to check that your ambitions are rightly motivated?

CHAPTER 23

WARNINGS

1. *Warnings can be as blunt as a sledgehammer and we still turn our heads and whistle them away.*

A. Give an example of a time when you ignored a warning and paid the price for it.

B. In addition to the passages Max mentions, what warnings does Proverbs offer about laziness (10:4–5; 12:11, 24); stinginess (11:24–26, 28; 19:17); and self-control (12:16, 23; 20:25; 21:23)?

C. In looking through Proverbs, what other warnings do you see occurring frequently?

D. Are there warning lights that you have been ignoring? about your health? your relationships with family or friends? your relationship with God?

E. If you were to write a proverb of warning for people today, what would you warn them about?

2. *We're often surprised at life's mishaps, but when pressed against the wall of honesty we have to admit that…we could have avoided many problems.*

A. Do you agree that we could avoid many of the mishaps in our lives? What kinds of mishaps are preventable? Why are we reluctant to admit that there have been warning signs?

B. Perhaps one of the best known examples of a person ignoring a warning is the story of Peter's denial of Jesus. Read the account in Matthew 26:31–46, 69–75 or in one of the other Gospels. How did Peter respond to Jesus' warning? Why? What made him deny Jesus even after being warned?

C. What lessons can we learn from Peter's experience that would help us heed the warnings we are given?

CHAPTER 24

FATHER'S DAY:
A TRIBUTE

1. *It seems strange that he isn't here. I guess that's because he was never gone. He was always close by. Always available.*

    A. What images come to mind when you think of your dad? What words would you use to describe him as a father?

    B. What God-given role are fathers to play in the lives of their children? What do these passages reveal: Deuteronomy 6:4–9; Psalm 78:1–8; Proverbs 3:11–12; Proverbs 13:24; Proverbs 22:6; Ephesians 6:4; 1 Timothy 3:1–5; 1 Timothy 5:8?

    C. In order to fulfill those responsibilities, what three factors would be most critical?

    D. What positive influences did your dad have on your life? If he is still alive, how could you express your appreciation to him for those things? If he isn't, to whom could you pass on those blessings?

2. *He is still…in a special way, very present.*

    A. If you have lost a parent or some other close family member, in what way is that person still very present with you?

    B. What does your family do to keep the loved one's memory alive? What makes those memories joyous rather than sad?

C. Why do you suppose God describes himself as our father? What fatherly characteristics do you see in these passages: Isaiah 64:8; Matthew 7:11; Matthew 10:29–31; 2 Thessalonians 2:16–17?

D. How does your faith affect your acceptance of the death of a loved one?

FAMILY SEDANS OF THE FAITH

1. *Reliability is the quality that produces not momentary heroics but monumental lives.*

> A. Which has more appeal to us—to be considered heroic or reliable? Why? To what extent does Christianity call us to be heroic? To what extent does Christianity call us to be reliable?

> B. Even though little is said about Andrew, what do you learn about him in each of these instances: John 1:35–42; 6:1–11; 12:20–22?

> C. Anna is mentioned only in Luke 2:36–38, yet those verses sum up the eighty years of her life. In what ways was she remarkably reliable?

> D. How would you rate your own reliability? How reliable are you in bringing others to Christ, like Andrew? How reliable are you in prayer, like Anna?

2. *I'm wondering if this book has found its way into the hands of some contemporary saints of reliability. If such is the case I can't resist the chance to say two things. The first? Thank you.*

> A. Within your own church what examples do you see of people who are models of reliability in their service to God? Where is their work generally done—"on stage" or "behind the scenes"? How are lives affected by their reliability?

B. Another word for "reliable" can be "faithful." How does Matthew 24:45–51 describe the faithful and unfaithful servants? What will be their end?

C. The faithfulness of God is a familiar theme throughout the Bible. Read Psalm 117. In what ways will God be faithful forever?

D. What could you do to thank or honor the "family sedans" within your church and to encourage others to be even more reliable?

INSENSITIVE SLURS

1. *If someone hurts your feelings intentionally you know how to react. You know the source of the pain. But if someone accidentally bruises your soul, it's difficult to know how to respond.*

when in a group

A. How do you respond if someone intentionally attacks you or your family or your friends? How do you respond if someone accidentally hurts you? Do you acknowledge it or ignore it? Can you slough it off or does the pain linger?

B. What wisdom do the following verses provide in responding to insults, intentional or not: Proverbs 19:11; Ecclesiastes 7:21–22; Luke 11:4; Luke 17:3–4; and 1 Corinthians 4:12–13?

C. To what extent does it matter if the attacker asks for for- ✓ giveness? How are we to respond if he asks for forgiveness? If he doesn't?

2. *He who dares to call himself God's ambassador is not afforded the luxury of idle words.*

A. Give an example of an instance in which you accidentally hurt someone by what you said.

B. Read Matthew 12:33–37. What is meant by "careless" words? What does this passage mean?

C. Read Proverbs 10:1–32. What contrasts are there between the words of the wicked and the words of the righteous?

D. What is the best advice you can give for using our words to God's glory?

CHAPTER 27

A SONG
IN THE DARK

1. *The passersby had various reactions. Some were curious and gazed unabashedly. Others were uncomfortable.... Most, however, hardly noticed him.*

✓ A. In which category do you fall? When confronted with someone like the blind beggar, are you curious, uncomfortable, or generally oblivious? Why?

✓ B. Are you reluctant to get involved, to get too close to the situation? Why or why not?

C. What was Jesus' response anytime people tried to shield him from others in need? How did he respond to the blind man (Mark 10:46–52); the children (Mark 10:13–16); the Canaanite woman (Matthew 15:21–28); Lazarus (John 11:1–16)? Why did Jesus' followers try to keep these people from him?

D. What can be done individually and as a church not to "pass by" those in need?

2. *Someone had told him, or maybe he'd told himself, that tomorrow's joy is fathered by today's acceptance. Acceptance of what, at least for the moment, you cannot alter.*

✓ A. Where is the right balance between accepting difficult circumstances and striving to improve them?

B. A striking example in the Bible of a person accepting what he could not change was Paul. Read 2 Corinthians 12:7–10. Why was Paul given the thorn in the flesh? How easily did he accept it? How did he use it for good?

C. Paul wrote to the Philippians apparently after he had been given the thorn in the flesh. What do we learn from Philippians 4:10–13 about his attitude of acceptance? What made Paul able to accept adversity?

D. What does Philippians 4:4–9 teach us about how to find joy even in difficult circumstances?

CHAPTER 28

IN THE MUD
OF JABBOK

1. *The best way to deal with our past is to hitch up our pants, roll up our sleeves, and face it head on.*

   A. What happens when we try to ignore the past? What does Max mean by facing it "head on"? How is that different from dwelling on the past?

   B. Read Genesis 32:1–33:3. Why did Jacob fear meeting Esau again? How did Jacob face the situation head on?

   C. How can we wrestle with God in dealing with our past? In what way might we also carry a limp?

2. *And for you who wonder if you've played too long to change, take courage from Jacob's legacy. No man is too bad for God.*

   A. Have you ever talked with someone who believed he or she had lived too bad a life to be accepted by God? What did you say to them?

   B. To get a picture of Jacob, the "riverboat gambler," read Genesis 27:1–45. What character traits does he exhibit?

   C. Yet, at the end of his life, what promise does God make to Jacob in Genesis 46:2–4? What blessings came through the descendants of Jacob?

D. What passages would you recommend to someone who is struggling with God's ability and willingness to forgive? Consider Isaiah 55:6–7; 1 Timothy 1:13–16; and 1 John 2:1–2.

E. Read Psalm 78, which describes Israel's relationship with God. How many examples does it give of God's provision for Israel despite their rejection of him? In one sentence, what is the message of this psalm?

A LITTLE BIT OF HANGIN'

1. *His aim is deadly. His goal is nothing less than to take what is most precious to us and make it appear most common.*

   A. What things are easiest for us to take for granted? A mate? Children? Health? God's love? Our lives? The future? Our salvation?

   B. Are those who have grown up believing in God at greater risk for taking their salvation for granted? In your experience, who seems most susceptible to becoming apathetic?

   C. What happens when we take our salvation for granted and become mediocre? What warning was given to the church in Ephesus that had lost its original love for Christ (Revelation 2:2–5)? What warning was given to the church in Laodicea for being lukewarm (Revelation 3:14–22)?

   D. How can we keep from taking for granted that which is precious? As Max put the picture of Jenna on his desk, what reminder of "the precious" could you put in front of yourself?

2. *The stool was kicked out from under my feet and the rope jerked around my neck just long enough to remind me of what really matters. It was a divine slap, a gracious knock on the head, a severe mercy.*

   A. What is meant by a "severe mercy"? Have you ever experienced a "severe mercy," "a divine slap"? What happened? How did it change you?

B.   In each of the following cases, how was a "divine slap" given: Jonah (Jonah 1–4); Zechariah (Luke 1:5–25, 57–80); Paul (2 Corinthians 12:7–10)? What benefit came from each?

C.   How can we learn to respond to difficulties as severe mercies rather than letting difficulties defeat us?

CHAPTER 30

CARMELITA

1. *We too were frightened orphans.... We too were rescued by a compassionate visitor, a generous parent who offered us a home and a name.*

    A. In what ways does the statement above aptly describe what God has done for us?

    B. To what is our relationship with God and Jesus compared in each of these passages: Isaiah 64:8; Psalm 95:6–7; 1 Peter 2:16; Romans 6:22; John 13:35? What different aspects of our relationship does each comparison point out?

    C. How do these passages describe our relationship to God and to Jesus: Romans 8:6–17; 1 John 2:28–3:10; Matthew 7:7–12? What is unique about being God's very children? What is significant about the phrase "Abba, Father" in Romans 8:15?

    D. In John 14:15–21, Jesus himself said he would not leave us as orphans. What did he promise those who love him?

    E. Is it hard to conceive of having the God of the universe as your own father? When do you feel closest to your heavenly father?

2. *We, too, should stand in the quiet company of him who saved us, and weep tears of gratitude and offer words of thankfulness. For it is not our bodies that have been rescued, but our souls.*

A. Have you ever witnessed a dramatic rescue? How did you feel?

B. According to the following passages, what are some of the things from which God has rescued us: Psalm 72:12–14; Romans 7:24–25; Titus 3:3–8; Colossians 1:13–14? How do we feel when we realize the fate from which we have been rescued? Compare the intensity of our emotions in a physical rescue with those in a spiritual rescue.

C. Read Revelation 7:9–17 and Psalm 8. What emotions do they capture? Spend a month reading the Psalms to focus on gratitude and praise for your salvation.

CHAPTER 31

SEEING THE SUMMIT

1. *Christianity, in its purest form, is nothing more than seeing Jesus.*

   A. What hinders us from seeing Jesus? Are we not looking? In what ways is he too obscure? In what ways is he perhaps too familiar?

   B. What promise is given to those who truly seek him? See Isaiah 55:6–7; Hebrews 11:6; Matthew 7:7–8.

   C. Has *God Came Near* helped you to see Jesus more clearly? If so, in what way? What new impressions do you take with you?

2. *Christian service, in its purest form, is nothing more than imitating him who we see.*

   A. If you could do only one thing to imitate Christ, what one thing would you choose to best depict Jesus to those who don't know him?

   B. According to Ephesians 5:1–2, what will characterize those who imitate Christ? By looking at the greater context of Ephesians 4:17–5:21, what else will be true of those who imitate Christ?

   C. What one area of your life could you work on this week to imitate Christ more closely?

"To see His Majesty and to imitate him, that is the sum of Christianity."
May this book and this Bible study have helped you to see His Majesty
more clearly and to imitate him more fully.

NOTES

Chapter 1
1. Luke 1:33

Chapter 2
1. Mark 12:31
2. Mark 10:29
3. Matthew 5:44
4. Matthew 28:20
5. 1 Corinthians 15:51–52, NKJV

Chapter 9
1. Colossians 4:11
2. Acts 13:6
3. Matthew 27:17; William Barclay, *Jesus As They Saw Him* (Grand Rapids, Mich.: Wm. B. Eerdmans).
4. Matthew 1:21
5. Hebrews 4:15

Chapter 10
1. Luke 7:11–17
2. John 4:1–42
3. Luke 8:43–47

Chapter 11
1. Mark 7:31–35
2. Romans 8:22–27

Chapter 13
1. 1 Corinthians 15:21–22, TEV

Chapter 14
1. Acts 2:22–23

2. Isaiah 53:10
3. Luke 9:51
4. John 10:17–18
5. John 6:61–62
6. Luke 13:32
7. Luke 9:31
8. John 1:29
9. John 10:15
10. Matthew 16:21
11. Matthew 21:42
12. Mark 14:3–9
13. John 13:27–30

Chapter 15
1. Psalm 139:7–8

Chapter 16
1. Luke 24:13–24

Chapter 19
1. Hebrews 8:12, RSV
2. Psalm 103:12
3. Hebrews 8:12, RSV
4. Isaiah 1:18, TLB
5. Galatians 3:27, RSV (italics mine)

Chapter 22
1. Genesis 11:4, RSV (italics mine)

Chapter 23
1. Proverbs 26:17
2. Proverbs 6:26–29, TLB
3. Hebrews 2:1
4. Galatians 6:7
5. Proverbs 21:19, NKJV

6. Proverbs 26:22
7. 1 Corinthians 15:33
8. Matthew 10:33
9. Proverbs 23:13–14, NKJV
10. Proverbs 19:27, NKJV
11. Proverbs 6:23, NKJV
12. Proverbs 13:10

Chapter 25
1. *Inside Sports* (September 1986), 10.
2. John 1:42; 6:8–9; 12:21–22
3. Philippians 2:25–30; 4:18

Chapter 26
1. James 3:6
2. Proverbs 21:23
3. Proverbs 13:3
4. Proverbs 10:19

Chapter 28
1. Genesis 32

Chapter 31
1. Philippians 3:19, Phillips
2. John 1:14, Phillips
3. 2 Peter 1:16b, RSV
4. John 3:3

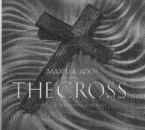
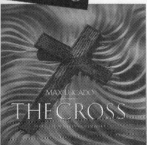